Top Trainers T

Starting a Sheepdog

Training a Border Collie on Sheep and Other Livestock

Edited by Sally Molloy and Heather L. Nadelman

Bill Berhow • Kate Broadbent • Carol Campion • Scott Glen

Bobby Henderson • David Henry • Julie Hill • Carla King

Kathy Knox • Lyle Lad • Beverly Lambert • Amanda Milliken

Barbara Ray • Derek Scrimgeour • Patrick Shannahan

Jeanne Weaver • Tom Wilson

OUTRUN PRESS

ISBN-13: 978-0-9794690-1-5

ISBN-10: 0-9794690-1-5

Library of Congress Control Number: 2007940782

PREFACE

This book grew out of our ongoing desire to understand as much as possible about transforming a young border collie puppy from its earliest days into a finished product capable of being useful around livestock and even running an Open course successfully. We have been interviewing sheepdog trainers for the past two years: our first interview was with Bobby Henderson in October 2005; our final one was with Kate Broadbent in August 2007. We tried to ask each person we interviewed roughly the same protocol of questions, so the similarities and differences in approaches would emerge clearly. Before we started the project, we were a bit concerned that the interviews could end up sounding too similar to one another: might it not be the case that the best trainers follow an essentially identical course when bringing their young dogs along? How different were they in process and approach? Is it simply the case that the best trainers merely have better timing than the rest of us, but that all are following the same general method?

We need not have worried. The trainers we talked to are alike in many respects: all have a deep understanding of young dogs and livestock, all were engaging to talk with and gracious about sharing their knowledge, and all have been remarkably successful in bringing out the talents of the dogs that they have trained. Yet many of the day-to-day details of exactly what they do and when they do it have diverged in ways that we at least have found fascinating. We hope that you find these interviews as enjoyable to read as we found them to transcribe, and we hope that you also find, as we did, some practical tips that will help you in the training of your own sheepdog hopefuls.

Contents

Bill Berhow

ZAMORA, CALIFORNIA

Bill Berhow has been training and trialing working border collies for the past thirty years. He is perhaps best known as the partner of his famous dog Nick, who was the USBCHA/ABCA National Finals champion three times, in 1989, 1990, and 1993. In 2007, Bill's dog Pete was both the CBCA National Champion and the winner of the prestigious Soldier Hollow Invitational Trial.

"I don't really start formal training until the dogs are pretty solidly ready for Open. I do a lot of real work with my dogs, and I let the work train the pup."

How long have you been involved in sheepdog training and trialing? How did that involvement first come about?

I've been training sheepdogs for about 28 years, and trialing for about 25. I had sheep and cattle when I was in college, and before—I grew up with them. So the first dog I had was an extension of that, really, but it was an untrained dog. I saw my first trial at Auburn University, and I was amazed at how much control they had, and how much more you could do with a dog when it was trained. And I guess ever since then it's been downhill!

Where did you get your first dog?

From a woman in Gainesville, Florida. I had cross- bred dogs before, but my first border collie came from Gainesville.

Did you train that dog yourself?

Oh, yes. I've trained all my dogs myself.

Did you have any help with them?

At that time down in Florida, you couldn't get any help. The fellas down here were using yellow curs and even Dobermans on cattle to get them out of the brush, and there just weren't many border collies at all. Most of the folks saw a border collie and just thought it was a mutt—they didn't know what it was. So there was absolutely no "help" anywhere, at least not that I knew of, since I didn't run in those sheepdog circles at the time. I knew something about livestock, and basically it was just a lot of trial and error and mistakes. I muddled my way through until I met certain folks who straightened me out.

Are you currently taking in young dogs for training, or are most of the dogs you start for your own purposes?

Both. I take about four or five dogs a month in for training—
no more than that. If you take more than that, I don't feel
that you can form the bond that needs to be formed. These
dogs don't work just because they're keen and have the instinct to do it. They work *for* somebody, because of a relationship. For me, the relationship they have with the trainer
is very important. So, if you keep more than about four dogs,
I don't think you have the time to supply that relationship.
And, of course, I always have a few young ones of my own
getting started.

How many dogs do you start a year, on average?

Not including my own, just client dogs could easily be sixty to
eighty dogs a year.

*What do you look for when you're choosing a puppy for
yourself?*

I'll be quite honest with you—I've never really picked a puppy
out of a litter. They've always been picked for me.

Who does that picking?

Oh, whoever's supplying the puppy, usually.

So you don't breed?

I breed a litter about every other year for myself, and usually
I end up with the puppy that wasn't chosen. Since I only
breed for myself, I'll often keep three or four out of the litter,
and give a couple to friends who are going to do right by the
dog. So I usually let them pick what they want. My grand-
father told me that he always picked the runt. Later, my
mother told me that he picked the runt because it was the only one he couldn't sell.

So you don't have strong feelings about what sorts of pups turn into the best sheepdogs?

Well, I like bold pups, very interested pups, very curious pups. I gravitate toward males, but I couldn't tell you why. It just seems to be what I like.

How are your pups raised? Are they house dogs?

Oh, yes. They're raised in and out of the house with me—they bump around with me. I don't go to a lot of trials anymore, but when I do they usually travel with me. If they're not old enough to train, I let them follow me around when I'm with the stock. When they start getting interested, I put them up so they won't get hurt. That's usually at around four months old; it's about that time that the world kind of turns for them. But before they're that age, I definitely let them come with me as much as possible.

Do they go into the kennel at some point?

It's about fifty-fifty—some of them will stay with me. The one that I have now is in and out of the house, and I don't think I'll put him in the kennel. But the four that I kept before did go into the kennel once they were ready to start training, for convenience and for separation. I think it's good to have a little bit of separation between the dogs and us at that point. They can start to read us a little too much, which sometimes means that they can anticipate our moves and moods a little too much. You want a little bit of mystery in there; I want to know the young dog, how he's going to react, but sometimes if we're around them too much, it's just too much of a good thing. We put them here and order them there, when what they need to be doing is feeling the world out a little bit. I also don't like them running loose and forming bad habits, and I don't like them running in a pack with each other.

What do you think happens if they run in a pack with each other?

They become less responsive to people. I want them thinking about me, not each other.

Do you have any feelings about the age that you'd like to see a pup show interest in sheep?

I'd like them to show pretty keen interest at about five months. I'm not afraid to wait to start training until twelve to fourteen months, but after that, I get a bit worried. Sometimes, if I really believe in a pup's breeding, and maybe I've seen pups bred the same way that have turned out well, and that pup wasn't completely turned on, I might send them to a friend's place for a couple of months, just to see if a change of environment and habit might spark a pup that's not quite going yet. But it's not generally a problem that I have. And pretty much, if a pup isn't working by the age of two, I'm going to be moving it on to a pet home of some sort.

What exactly do you mean here by "working"?

Just showing enough interest to be trained.

What do you consider the ideal age to begin formal training of a pup?

I don't really start "formal" training at any time until the dogs are pretty solidly ready for Open. I do a lot of real work with my dogs, and I let the work train the pup. That dog could easily be two years old before I really do any formal training. But at that time, it will know how to cast for sheep over distances, it'll know how to flank, it'll know how to walk into the stock, and how to drive, before I do any formal training.

So how exactly are you defining "formal training"?

Strict adherence to commands.

So when you're teaching, say, a flank, you're not insisting on absolute obedience in the beginning?

I'm just putting a label on what the dog is already doing— usually the sheep and the situation tell the dog how to flank and where to flank. I like taking a young dog out around a big flock just to move the flock across the pastures and let the dog have fun with it. But I don't consider that formal training. Formal training is really preparatory work for trialing. If a dog can't do useful work for me, I'm not going to go ahead and train it for the trial field, because it'll let me down there.

What kind of place do you have for training your dogs?

I have 180 acres on my home farm, and then I lease another 100 acres. It's very rolling and hilly.

What sort of sheep do you have?

Several hundred Cheviots, Scottish Blackface, some St. Croix, and then some other wool breeds. I'm new to the area, so I'm trying to find the sheep that work best for where I am now. I haven't yet figured that out—it might be that the Katahdins and St. Croix are what I need. The Scotties hold up really well. The Cheviots have a really hard time with the heat: I love Cheviots, but I think I'm going to need to eliminate them from the program. I don't really like hair sheep for training—I don't think they put much power and connection into a dog. But they're certainly very economical in the heat.

Do you ever start your pups on any livestock other than sheep?

I started with cattle, and I wouldn't be afraid to start them on some nice lightweights. But if you're going to use cattle, you just need to be that much more knowledgeable about stock and dogs to start them correctly. If the dogs aren't started correctly, if they're started too young, you end up with dogs that are too eager to use their teeth—they resort to that first before resorting to eye.

Do you teach your pups any commands before you introduce them to stock?

They learn to come when they're called—that's about it. Maybe I should do more with "lie down" and "stay" and the like, but they seem to know my voice anyway. When I walk through a gate and tell the pup "stay—you stay," they seem to know what I mean. So I guess you might say that I teach that too, but it's not really an active, conscious thing. I just find it's a lot easier to train on the sheep than off the sheep. When I start putting a down on a dog, I find that it's easier to do on the sheep, because the sheep bring that stop out in them. It's just a lot easier and a lot less pressure.

What sort of sheep, and how many sheep, do you like to use for starting your pups?

It depends. I might start them on the whole flock—I might move a couple of hundred head of sheep around with pups, and I'll vary it. As the pup starts getting a little more precise in his work, I'll start bringing the numbers down. It really depends on the dog and what kind of eye it appears he's going to have and what kind of movements he's going to have. If he's real brash and rough in his work I'll keep him on a lot of sheep, to let him work all that brashness out. When that young dog is in there grabbing a sheep, it's also getting yanked around by the sheep, it's hurting, and it doesn't feel good. The sheep pretty much teach the dog how to be careful and how to behave themselves. If the dogs are overworking themselves with that type of behavior, they'll realize pretty quickly that they're going to run out of energy.

Your system is fairly unusual, isn't it?

When these dogs were developed by the old master stock-men, there were no trials. The way they trained their dogs fit the form and the mental abilities of the dogs. So I believe in training them for the function for which they were originally developed, and I train a little differently from many people. My dogs might be driving and sorting out sheep, for instance, long before they ever have a down on them. And with the larger numbers of sheep and the open spaces that I have, I don't usually run into any problems.

So you don't ever use a round pen to help you start your pups?

No, I never use a round pen. I might have an older dog out there, to help me keep things in check. But the great thing about dog training is that, if something falls apart, I can just call the pup back to me and start again. You haven't lost the moment—you can just set it up and do it again.

So you expect your pups to be able to be called off the sheep from the beginning?

Oh, yes. I insist on it. If they don't do that right away, I stay with them until they do. I may have to take them to the sheep on a rope, but normally coming off I don't need any sort of a leash. One of the things that I'm firm about is that I don't want the pup going to sheep except when I say: I want them to start and stop on my word. But I don't like to use ropes or leashes or any other aids, and I get away from those as quickly as I can manage it.

So you don't use any training aids, like a pole or a rattle paddle?

No. I carry a crook, of course—I'd feel naked without it. But every tool you use diminishes your reasoning ability, your logic and stock sense, and it also diminishes the dog. So I avoid them. The only tool I'd ever recommend, and that's only for people who really need it, is a long rope. If someone has a dog that won't come off sheep, or is just a bit too anxious or unruly, I do recommend a long rope, even though I don't use it on my own dogs.

What do you like to see in a pup's first few sessions on sheep?

A strength of focus on the work and on the sheep, and a direct approach to the sheep. When I first take a pup to sheep, I watch how much control they have over themselves. If they have enough—maybe within a fifty percent parameter—I go right ahead and put them to work. But if the first thing the pup does is to charge through the sheep and lose its head completely and shut me out entirely, then I know that the dog is too young for training, and I'll try it again in another month or two. If you're lucky, the dog will cast out and release the sheep nicely from his eye. I like forward dogs—everything should always be forward. I don't mind a pup with teeth, because they seem to work that out on their own. I don't mind things like running through sheep or grabbing at something, because I know that they're just things that puppies tend to do. I let them know that it isn't acceptable, but I don't make a huge issue over it. I want that pup to know first and foremost, even if things aren't starting out very well, that it's the best thing in the world and that *I'm* the best thing in the world. Whether the pup is right or wrong, whether I'm mad at it or not, I want that pup to be very confident in itself.

No matter what happens, I want the dog to have a very positive attitude toward itself and toward me. At that point, I don't want that dog to have any fear of me, or any fear of making a mistake. If it's afraid of making a mistake, it'll often hesitate in its work, and I don't like dogs who hesitate too much. I like dogs that are really forward, who are always thinking and always trying. They can always learn the correct thing to do over time, but the first priority is that the dog tries.

What would you not like to see in the first couple of sessions? What behaviors might warn you of later problems?

Maybe a pup that's *real* sticky, with so much eye that it won't release sheep. A dog that's lackadaisical about its work and that would rather be off doing something else. If I see a dog that loses its head easily, that tells me that I have to be very careful in the way I approach it. I don't want to put it over its head or get it into the habit of working over its head. If dogs get into a pattern of working when their minds are chaotic, that can be a problem that's difficult to get rid of. But I also don't want to keep the dog from that chaos by control—I want to put them into situations that allow them to get over it on their own. If I'm controlling the chaos, that chaos is still in the dog—all it's going to know is how to stop or go right or go left when it's told, but it's not going to know how to settle its own mind unless it's learned to do that, and that's not something that I can teach it to do—the sheep have to teach them that, and it's probably one of the harder things to get through to them.

How do you go about doing it?

Well, the best young dogs are really hard when you start them, in willpower and initiative. The best ones have a lot of initiative, and their approach is very forward. Some of those dogs can get in over their heads pretty quick. I don't want them to be in over their experience level very often. If I see that they are (while moving the flock around or something), I'll pretty quickly get in there and change the situation so that they're not in it anymore, so they can learn that when they work they want to keep their heads collected. And the dogs that I end up trialing *do* manage to keep their heads collected under often very difficult situations.

Can you think of a dog that you trained that started really easily? And did that dog continue to become an outstanding dog after it was finally trained? In general, do you think that the dogs who train up really easily tend to be the best dogs in the end?

My old Tweed dog trained up really easily, and he ended up being a very good dog. What I've found is that the dogs who train up the quickest using the sort of approach that I like to use tend to be the cream of the crop.

On average, how long would it take you to get a dog to Nursery level?

That depends so much on the dog that I really couldn't give you an answer to that one. It depends on how they accept the work. Believe it or not, if you start the dog at the right age, it could take as little as three or four weeks, but it also could be as long as five or six months. It's really hard to say. And some of them that take even longer, like a year or even two, are worth waiting on, and a good dog person will know which ones are worth the wait and time.

How much time do you like to give dogs before deciding that they're not worth the wait and the time?

In all honesty, I just don't come across that many dogs that I'd want to give up on. The issue with me is that I sell so many young dogs that a lot of them I don't keep long enough to decide that they're not worth it. If I sell the dog, that means that I think it's worth continuing with, or else I'd just find it a pet home. The started dogs that I sell can gather sheep and are started on driving, and they know how to flank pretty well. They may or may not have a stop on them, since a stop is way down the line in what I teach.

When do you first introduce the stop? And how do you introduce it?

I tend to wait until the dog stops of its own accord, and then I just put a label on the behavior. And that may happen right away—it might be the first time that that the dog is on the sheep. Now, when I *insist* on it is something else again—there's a good chance that that won't happen until the dog is at Pro-Novice level. I want them to have a good solid "go" before I insist on a good solid "stop."

Do you insist that your dogs lie down on their bellies?

That depends on the dog. If a dog will stand quietly on his feet, I let him stay there. But if he goes to stop on his feet but comes pushing out toward the sheep, then I'll take him off his feet. If he's an overly aggressive dog, I might take him off of his feet to give him a chance to stop quietly. But if he can stop quietly on his feet without taking advantage of the sheep or of the situation, I'll leave it alone.

How about the steady command and pace in general? Where does that fit in?

It seems to introduce itself when I'm using the larger bunch of sheep and just moving the sheep along. I might say the dog's name a little sharply if he's moving them too quickly, to slow him up. If I decide that I want to move onto trialing work with that particular dog, then I'll start to put a command on the nice pace. The problem is that if you try to put too much pace on a dog too early, you lose the power and confidence in the dog. So my dogs might actually be running in Open before I really start to put a steady command on them. My dog Pete is one of the best dogs that I've had, and he actually had won Open trials before he got any strict, formal training in pace.

So did you just rely on the stop command with him?

No, I just relied on his own common sense—or his name, to check him up. I've seen too many dogs who had the steady put on them too soon and who lost power because of it. However, it can be a different story if you have a really aggressive or willful dog. I believe that all of these dogs need to learn certain things at certain times, "stop" being one of those things, and power and confidence being another. If you don't learn those lessons at the right window, it's very hard to learn them later on.

Tell me a little about your training progression: what do you like the dog to master first before you move on to the next thing, and so on?

I don't have a progression in that way—I kind of start with it all. I do want the dog to have self-control before I start using it to sort stock, but that dog might not even be driving before I start using it to shed sheep and sort out sheep. The outrun is one of the last things that I try to perfect, and I really don't work on that for quite a long time. I do like a dog to know to check up on its name before I start working on driving. But nothing in my training is really structured until I decide that I may want to use a dog for trial work, and then I'll start structuring things a little more. But the dog could easily be two and a half years old before that happens.

And what do you do at that point, when you decide that you want to work on the dog for trials?

I ask for a little more perfection in the dog's work, a little more obedience, a little more precision in how he handles fewer head of sheep. At a certain age, I may even put that dog on a single sheep: that's great work for a dog to help develop real precision, and it brings out a lot of the dog's natural stock sense. Most of the dogs that I develop aren't very sticky, because of the way that I train, but working a single sheep can help test a dog that might be a little too sticky, and help him work out releasing pressure when he's told to do that.

How do you go about stretching a dog's outrun?

I always have a certain type of work that needs to be done—say, that these sheep need to be gathered in those hills. I don't make the work any easier, because the work still needs to be done. But what I do is to insert myself more and more into the situation, depending on how green the dog is. I want to limit my input as much as I can, whatever we're doing, but I'll do what the dog needs done depending on his level of training. I do think that a good dog will know what has to be done but will also do what he's told.

Since you start your dogs emphasizing the work rather than "formal" training, do you ever find that your dogs have developed any bad habits when you start to polish them for trials?

No, not at all—just about the opposite, really. I find that with a well-bred dog I hardly need to do any polishing at all. When the time comes to lock the dogs in for trial work, there's maybe ten percent of the work left to do.

When do you start introducing whistles?

As soon as I can. I use a call-off whistle almost immediately, and the stop and walkup whistles are almost a given to all of them. As soon as I see that the dog is checking itself up, I'll start using a stop whistle there. It's like kids learning language—they learn it so much more quickly than adults would. So I want my dogs learning whistles young, when they can accept it more easily.

Do you ever use different whistles for different kinds of dogs?

Yes. If a dog has flanks that are more open and controlled, I might give that dog a quicker, sharper kind of whistle. If a dog is flanking too abruptly, I'd give it a drawn-out sort of whistle.

How do you go about starting the drive?

I just walk behind the sheep with the dog. I've got one now that's fighting it quite a bit, who really wants to flank a lot. I just keep walking behind the sheep with him and pulling him into me.

How large a group of sheep do you use?

That depends on the dog, but anywhere from fifty to two hundred.

Are you doing that in an open field?

Everything I do is in an open field. I find that fences can introduce some bad habits to dogs, making them want to hook around and hold sheep to the fence. So I don't use fences at all in my training. But they can be helpful for people who aren't reading the reactions of the sheep quickly enough, or who don't have extensive experience with livestock.

What do you do about pups who want to grip, or who single one sheep off and chase it?

As far as the gripping goes, I like to let the pup work that out for itself. I'll let them know that it's wrong and shame them a little bit for doing it, but I won't run at them. All dogs grip from pressure, either pressure from us, from the sheep, or from the situation, so what I try to do is to eliminate enough of that pressure. If, for instance, the pressure is from the sheep (either because they're too tough or because they're running too fast), I don't want to chase that dog or throw things at it, because I'm just introducing more pressure into the situation. All my dogs seem to work out the gripping and chasing in the end; I've had very few who haven't. As far as cutting off a single sheep and working it, I've found that some border collies seem quite keen to do that sort of thing. I try to look at the sheep and anticipate when it might happen, such as when the flock I'm working with starts to spread out and thin at the ends and the dog wants to cut into that little thin part. I'll try to anticipate that and take a little more control of the situation, maybe by moving into the dog or moving into where that peak of sheep is starting to point, so that the dog is more inclined to stay on the outside of the sphere of the sheep, rather than cutting in.

How do you go about teaching shedding?

I just use a large bunch of sheep, and when I get a natural break I'll call the dog through to me. If possible, the dog and I will then walk those sheep off. If that's not possible, if the sheep are trying to break back to the others, I'll move around to the fetch side and let the dog fetch the sheep to me.

How much do your dogs tend to know before you start shedding with them?

When I start with them on shedding, they know to stay out of the sheep fairly well, and they pull up when they hear their names fairly well too. Of course, the more they know, the less work it is to train them. For instance, it's not essential that the dog know a stop to learn to shed, but it makes the task easier for me.

I have to say again that I find most of the dogs today so well bred, from almost all lines, that the task of training them is really quite easy. And that's even the case with most of the dogs that I run, who are pretty tough dogs—I like a hard, tough dog. But what I *don't* do with dogs is set up any sort of confrontation between the dog and me. We don't have a con-frontational sort of relationship; what I'm trying to do all the time is to set up a working partnership.

How do you avoid getting into confrontations with your dogs?

I don't play the game with it—if the dog wants to fight with me, I just don't do it. I either take the dog off the sheep, or if I find myself getting tense and frustrated, that's telling me that I'm going off in the wrong direction, and I'll stop the session right there. Once I start playing the "you're not going to beat me" game with the dog, I've lost.

So you don't believe that a training session always needs to end on a good note?

No. I'll just stop. I let the dog know that I still think the world of it, even if it hasn't done well on that particular day. I want the dog to think the world of itself, because I know that to-morrow is another day.

What if a dog did something really egregious, like taking down a sheep?

I'd get after it, certainly—I'd shame it, and let it know that it had done something terrible. But once it had accepted that correction, I'd let it get right back to work. If it repeated it, I'd do the same thing, maybe this time even a little firmer. But if I'm feeling too grouchy in a training session, or if a dog is too young for what I'm trying to do with it, I just shut things down right then and there and wait until I'm in a better frame of mind or maybe until the dog's a little bit older.

What do you like to get out of the first trials that you enter your young dogs in?

With young dogs, I'm certainly not out to win the class—I'm just there for the experience, and so I can see what the dog is going to do on different fields and different sheep. But before I go to a trial I try to work the dog in as many different conditions, with as many different kinds of sheep, as possible. I definitely want to expose them to someone spotting the sheep, so they can get experience with that. But normally when I start to run a dog in trials, I'll have it just about ready for Open—we'll normally only be in Pro-Novice for a couple of runs before I move the dog up to Open.

How do you feel about the Nursery program?

It's a great program—it's very good for the dogs, and it's proven itself over the years. We have more good young dogs now than I ever remember seeing before. If there's any problem with the program, it's us—we train them too far, too fast, just for the program. But that's our fault, not the fault of the program. It's gotten more people training their own dogs and doing it themselves than anything else.

What's the most important thing you'd like to tell people who are trying to train a dog for the first time?

I was always obsessed with these dogs, not just about trialing, but about the dogs themselves. I remember that Ralph Pulfer was once asked what he thought my most valuable trait as a trainer was, and he said "persistence." I believe that *is* a very valuable trait for any dog trainer: don't give up, be dogged. Any trainer is going to get frustrated, even the very best trainers. But if you're persistent, and if you believe in the dog, it'll make that dog. Persistence, sticking with it and listening, is really the key for any beginning trainer.

Kate Broadbent

NOVA SCOTIA, CANADA

Kate Broadbent spends her days as an itinerant shepherd and shearer, traveling throughout Canada and the United States helping with the running of various working sheep farms. In addition, she breeds and trains working border collies as well as competing successfully in some of the most prestigious trials in North America.

"Always remember that the dogs are trying their best to cue into *our* body language and *our* signals and *our* vocabulary."

How long have you been involved in sheepdogs?

I sort of grew up with dogs. I started working with sheepdogs when I went to New Zealand after graduating from college. That's where I saw working dogs being used really effectively. I was already interested in sheep and shearing, so I just progressed from there.

What made you decide to go to New Zealand? Was it to learn more about sheep?

I just really wanted to travel. I did a lot of traveling after college, and New Zealand was just one place that I really wanted to see. So I went, intending to stay six months. I ended up staying two years, and then I spent the next ten years going back and forth.

Do you currently take dogs in for training, or are you just starting dogs for yourself?

I do take them in for training infrequently, or help people out by tuning up their dogs for a couple of weeks at a time, but I prefer to train up dogs and sell them. I try to sell about three or four a year—it's part of what I do for a living.

When you're choosing a pup for yourself, what do you look for? When you look at a litter, how would you describe your ideal puppy?

I tend to consider the genetics of the litter—the parents—rather than the puppy itself. I often just tell people to pick me a pup and send it to me; sometimes I get the pup that nobody else wants. It's more the genetics and what I've seen in the parents that I'm interested in. I've had enough dogs that I can sort of pick through them; for instance, I know how much eye I like in a dog. I might be a little leery of a very shy pup in the litter, but that might be the one I end up with, and even that one can sometimes turn out to be a great one. I don't think you really *can* pick a puppy at six weeks of age. Maybe someone stood on that one's foot yesterday, and when you look at the litter it screams or runs away when you go to pick it up. Often if you isolate a puppy from the litter it changes, and it changes again at six months.

Now I know that you've said in the past that you like a little more eye in your dogs than some people are comfortable with. Do you think you can see that eye in a puppy from their behaviors apart from livestock?

No, you don't see that until you start the dog. They're all border collies—showing eye to a ball as a puppy doesn't really mean anything. I do like a really stylish dog, so my dogs tend to have a bit of eye. But I think I get away with it because I do so much big flock work with my dogs. I do very little schooling on three or four sheep. So my dogs don't get sticky—they have to flank, or we're not going to get anything done. So I don't think that I go *looking* for eye, but I seem to end up with it. And a lot of my dogs are quite forward and pushy, so the eye doesn't hold them up in any way. I wouldn't keep a dog that genuinely had too much eye, so much that it was making it sticky. But as far as predicting any of that in puppies, no, I can't see that kind of thing that early.

When you have pups, how are they raised? Are they house dogs or kennel dogs?

They're camper dogs! I live in a camper, and I'm on the road all the time, so they're with me. I try to raise only about one pup a year and not keep two from a single litter because I only have so much time to spend with a pup, and keeping more than one doesn't really work for me. (If I keep two pups, my limited time has to be divided in half.) But the pups are part of the pack from the beginning—I expect them to be quiet in their crates, and come when they're called, and all those sorts of things.

Are there any specific commands that you like to teach your pups before you take them to sheep for the first time?

No, I'm terrible about that. A lot of people do good obedience work with their pups, but I admit that I'm often a bit slack with it. I like the pups to be able to walk on a leash and to come when they're called, but I don't tend to work on a lie down or anything like that apart from the stock. I do try to teach my pups to learn, and to make sure that they're really keyed into me and what I want. Just the basic things that I do to make them nice dogs to be around is really teaching them how to learn, and how to accept a bit of discipline. That way, when you do take them to stock, that initial correction isn't going to blow their minds, because they've already had experience with a gruff tone of voice or a little bit of pressure on them. So they learn all the basic things: you don't jump up, or bark in your crate, and you come when you're called, and you walk on a leash—all of those sorts of things, I do. But I don't do a lot of formal obedience work with my pups.

So you're really just teaching your pups to have a relationship with you and to understand what a correction means?

Yes, absolutely. I get dogs in for training sometimes who have been absolutely spoiled and who have never been corrected. It can take two weeks with dogs like that just getting them to the point where they can take a correction without its ruining their day and forcing them to quit because they can't deal with it. I like my pups to understand when they're wrong and what to do about it.

When do you like your pups to start showing an interest in livestock?

I think we all get excited about that six-week or ten-week or three-month-old puppy that wants to work. I will expose them in a pretty controlled, quiet situation at around three months old, and if they don't show an interest I don't worry about it. We all like to see a young pup really keened in, but I don't worry about it much. I like to see a pup at six or eight months old showing some interest, even if it's just wanting to chase. But if the tail is up and they bark, I put them up for awhile. I've had a few really precocious ones who were ready to go very early, and that spoils you when you get a big dumb male who doesn't turn on until he's a year old. But, at the end of the day, that male might end up being the better dog. So I don't start doing much with a pup until about ten to twelve months old, when the pup is physically mature and mentally able to take a bit of pressure.

How exactly do you go about introducing your pups to live-stock?

For their first exposures, I like it to keep things calm. But, even saying that, I do take pups with me on the four-wheeler when I'm moving a few sheep or in the truck when we're feeding. So they've been around flocks of sheep, and if they take a little run at the sheep I don't worry about it. But if they're really keened up and getting into trouble I stop taking them along. I don't expect pups to train themselves, but I take them with me in these sorts of situations as much to have them be with me as to expose them to the sheep.

Is there an age that you think it might be too late to start a dog?

No; it just depends on how much time you want to put into it. Why would you want to put the time into a six-year-old when you could put that time into a twelve-month-old? There have been people who have had clinics where someone might bring a six-year-old flyball dog—they'll take it to sheep, it turns on, and they're thrilled. But they don't have any intention of making it into a trial dog. If it's there, it's there—it just depends on how much time you want to spend, and at what age.

Tell me more about the environment that you like to use to start a young dog.

When I'm ready to start a pup seriously (at approximately ten months or a year), I like to have a very controlled environment. I like something a bit bigger than a round pen, like a riding arena or a pen just big enough so that things are not going to get out of hand. The sheep can be pretty undogged, but I don't want sheep that are going to stamp and face a dog off right away—that might demoralize a young pup that might not initially have a lot of confidence. I like to use about half a dozen—maybe ten—sheep. The number doesn't really matter, but I want to do it in such a way that I can ask that pup to be correct. I'll let the crazy stuff go for a turn or two, but after that I want that pup to understand that I'm in the picture. Often these young pups will go to balance right away, but then I step in with a bit of pressure and ask the pup to give ground off of the sheep, and be workmanlike about it. I want to be right there every time, and in a small pen or arena you can do that; you can put the sheep on the fence and get in between the sheep and the pup. I don't let them have their sheep unless they're right, and that's something that I really advocate. I used to start them out in a field, where they'd flail around, chase, and slice and slice. We'd eventually get there— I think the real beauty of these dogs is that you can train them lots of different ways and get to a point where you can run them in an Open trial—but my preference now is to start them in a small area. By doing it that way, in thirty days or so I have a dog that I can use to set sheep with at a trial, if it's the right dog. It used to take me a lot longer, because the dog got into the habit of doing things that weren't acceptable. I can avoid all that by starting in a small area and teaching the pups correct behavior from the beginning.

When I leave the pen with a young dog, they're going to have a recall off the sheep, a stop, and a pretty good left and right flank. They'll also go all the way around the sheep off balance. I'll put a "there" command on them all around the clock, and they can stop and walk in at any of those points. I do drills that put quite a bit of pressure on the pups, but I also keep it fun: I'll call them around, say, to 9:00, and use a "there" to get them to walk in, and that's really the very beginning of driving. I'll even ask the pup to drive around the edges of our little arena before we step outside of it. I want the pup to understand some of the basics and be workmanlike about it. There might be wrecks with young dogs, but I don't want them to get away with chasing sheep; they need to understand that there is a certain way that we work the sheep all of the time. With young dogs, everything is habit: it's a lot easier to start with good habits right from the beginning than it is to break a bad habit. My dogs learn that if they give in to pressure from me, they get their sheep back right away. It's a way of training that suits me, and it also suits the type of dogs that I seem to like.

Do you ever use any livestock other than sheep to start your young dogs?

No, usually sheep. If I had some goats I'd use them, and I occasionally use calves—I like to know whether I've got a cattle dog or not.

Are there any particular training aids that you like to use?

No, not really. Every once in awhile I'll have a pup that really wants to be in tight on its sheep, and you need a bit of a crop or a buggy whip, just to make that shushing noise. But in general, I want them to give to me, not to an aid—I don't do the flags and the crooks and the canes or any of that. I used to do that—I used to pick up the big stick and look like a cavewoman running across the field to make them widen out. But I find that if I do it in a smaller area I can step in, get in that dog's eye, push it, and then give. But yes, once in awhile I'll want an aid that makes a bit of a pop to let them know that what I'm asking is for them to give off of me.

What do you like to see in a talented pup's first few sessions?

We all like that pup who just goes immediately into the corner after sheep and digs them out of it. But I really try not to judge too much by those first couple of sessions; if they bark and throw up their tails, they're not necessarily for sale. You need to give all of them a chance to develop their confidence. I've had dogs that were really silly and immature until they were about a year and a half old, and it took that long for them to develop confidence. But there are others that are just confident right away. I like to see "face"—I like a pup that will walk right into the face of sheep. If you see that in a youngster you're pretty excited about it. If I have a pup that's willing to walk into the face of sheep or pull sheep out of a corner, even if they bite a little and pull a bit of wool, even if they're a little afraid, it's a lot better than not trying. If, on the other hand, I have a pup that wants to quit when a sheep looks at him, I'm disappointed. If they get older and that sort of thing keeps up, I'd probably sell the dog.

Would anything other than not trying when a sheep looks at the pup warn you of later problems?

If the pup were really wide, I'd worry. If I saw a dog just giving, giving, giving to the sheep I'd be worried about that, because that's a hard one to fix. But with most of them, you give them a chance for a few times before really starting to analyze things like how much eye you think they're going to have. A clappy pup that just lies and watches, who needs a bit of movement from the sheep before wanting to get up, would concern me. But often you'll see a pup do that for the first session or two because they're just baffled—they really don't know what's going on here. But soon you might find that your encouragement has created a monster, and that they're ripping through the sheep so much that you need to stop encouraging them and get into the picture. By the time they're about a year old I like to be able to make an assessment, to know if a pup is really loose-eyed or has a good feel for the sheep or has too much eye.

Do any of the dogs that you've trained stand out in your mind as having been exceptionally easy to train? How did that dog turn out as a finished product?

My dog Rose was very precocious. She has too much eye and she can get a bit too wide, but she's been a relatively successful trial dog for me, as well as a good work dog and a good lambing dog. She's very smart and quick, and she really understands what I want from her. I've had a few of those very precocious ones over the years; I actually trained a Rose daughter who picked up her whistles in two days. But a lot of the slower learners and the slower maturers end up fine—they just take a little bit longer to get there.

Do you think that in general the precocious ones end up being the best dogs?

We have to pick the right puppy, we have to raise it right, we have to train it right, we have to not run over it with a tractor. The potential for human error in all of this is huge. But yes, if you have that quick, precocious pup that walks right into the face of sheep and learns like crazy, you're pretty excited about it, and you need to try not to screw it up. And it's always us who screw things up: we're imposing *our* rules on these dogs, and we're communicating with them on *our* terms, not theirs, and they're desperately trying to figure out what we want. So if things don't go right, it's us, not them. And sometimes we expect too much of dogs that just don't have the ability. You know, we are asking more of them in situations than they've actually got. I think that 99.9 percent of these dogs out here,

whether it is in a working situation or the trial field, are giving us their best. And when it doesn't work, we need to recognize that.

*After what age or what amount of time would you give
up on a pup that you thought was not progressing satisfactorily?*

Oh, I don't know. I guess it would depend how bad it was. I
don't really give up on them, they go for goose work, or they
go to a farm or ranch home if they aren't going to make that
high-end trial dog.

*Let's talk a little about your training program: what's your
general training progression? What skill do you like to start
with, or have dogs master before they go on to the next skill?*

It sort of depends on the dog because some show you a real
great feel and incredible balance right from the beginning,
and some are much looser-eyed and flop past balance. But
basically what I like to see when I start my pups is that willingness to learn, and attentiveness—they recognize that you
are on the team, they are working with you, they are looking
for direction. Because I start them in a smaller area, I'm introducing a lot of the different facets of work quite early on.
Of course, they've got to stop. I like a dog to stop on his feet. I
want them to flank cleanly without slicing the sheep. And I'm
working on all of those things right away. I'm not stretching
them out on outruns until they get out of this pen, and
they've been on sheep for 2 or 3 weeks, 4 weeks, 5 weeks
depending on the dog. What I'm looking for and what I'm
insisting on is stockmanship. They are not allowed to chase
sheep. We are not jamming them up the back, we are not

slicing sheep, we are not running through the middle. Every time they get to sheep, and as I'm working with them and giving them vocabulary—left and right and stuff, they must come on in a thoughtful way. We don't treat sheep poorly. You know, the first time or two, yeah, puppies are crazy, but after that we do it thoughtfully.

And what do you do if they don't?

You correct them. You get in there. They are not getting those sheep until they do it correctly. And then as you progress through, they are learning left and right. Some pups learn that really quickly, others take a lot more direction. Of course, my focus on it is that I want them to learn left and right, I don't want them to key up on my body language all the time—I start to phase that out right away. When I say "come-bye," I like to see that pup shift one way, then shift the other; I like to see that his brain is working, the wheels are spinning. Is it this one? Right, reward him, let him have those sheep, he's good. I want a good stop, a thoughtful stop. It's not an obedience thing, it's not "stop until I tell you to get up." It's "stop, good, now you can have your sheep again." Now it's a flank, now it's walk up. I tend not to put a big, hard down on them right away. I put a "there" on all of them, so they can turn in on the sheep and keep moving. Then introducing that stop and then getting to the point where you lie them down and they will steady, so you can go open the gate and the sheep can go through, or whatever.

As soon as I get them kind of broke so that I can control them, I take them to work. I start using them for little jobs. Following big groups of sheep down across the prairie down the road. Not hard stuff—not ewes and baby lambs, not pushing in the chutes on real tough sheep. Just gathering and getting a good feel for how well they are going to deal with those sorts of things. I feel that the sheep put enough pressure on the young dogs, so I don't have to. Once they've got the basics, I take them to work. Then they get a feel for sheep, they learn how to work sheep. The pressure of training comes later on as they get a bit more mature. You know, a dog that is 18 months old should be able to do a bit of work. He's got the basics, he knows how to work sheep and he's taken the pressure of the stock well enough. At this point, it's time for me to be able to put a bit of pressure and really fine-tune a lot of that training.

So you start with a stop by asking them to stop on their feet, and move to the lie down later. Are there some dogs you never actually ask to lie down?

They all have to get a lie down so they stop, but a lot of them will do it without asking, because if you stop them and make them stay, they'll lie down. When it is a situation where they've got it, everything is there, it's just a function of what we're doing. Stay on the bike, stay behind the horse, that sort of thing. And you've got to discipline them, of course, especially those pups that are up every time. But I do like a stand on a dog, I like a dog that stops on its feet, but that is just aesthetic.

What about pace?

Pace is how you work sheep. We don't rush around and chase them. We take our time, or else you don't get the sheep. And in that small area I find that I can just step in and get between them and the sheep and I can physically put some pressure on them, "I said slow down." And if you've got that all initially, I can often take a pup from a horse arena or from a small pen and send them 250 or 300 yards and they are right. Because the habit they have formed is that we are deep enough at the top, we break down and we think about what we are doing, we don't chase them. Some of them, the good natural ones, are amazing. You step out and say, "Oh, I think he can do it," and you just send him. I'm not saying he's trial ready, but he's got the work ethic, he understands how he is expected to behave.

Now are you just working on pace all of the time and instilling it as a habit, or do you put a word or a steady whistle on the dog so that you can ask them to notch it down when you need to?

I say steady and I have a steady whistle, and they had better notch it down when I ask for it. I want to see that break down in their stride. And they are so receptive to tone of voice that if they understand what you are asking and you can step in there and reinforce it every time—they get it. And that's not saying that it works all of the time. I've got a dog now that at 800 yards does not slow down the way I'd like him to.

When, if ever, do you insist on absolute obedience? And how do you balance absolute obedience with developing a pup's initiative and confidence?

Oh, you need the obedience right from the beginning, and that is, again, back to that small area. I've said stand and if he doesn't, I'm in his face, I'm right there. He'll stand. Good dog, let's go, have your sheep. I've got a steady whistle, but when I blow a stop he had better stop, because you need that. It is not, "Lie down, lie down, lie down," and they never lie down for me. It means something. And it has to because of the type of work I do. He's got to call off when I ask him to. Of course, with a pup taking wrong flanks you can't be savage with your corrections, but if you are there you give them a chance to key in on the verbal, and if he goes the wrong way you step in and you are correcting him. Just physically being there to tell him to go the other way, just a physical cue, which I try to rely on less and less right away so that he is listening instead of just waiting for me to lift a stick or move my arm or take a step. And it isn't authoritarian—you don't have to get in there and hit them. Every once in a while there is one that needs a bit more corporal punishment, something a bit more physical because they get a bit hot-headed and don't listen or don't stop. Again, if you start in a small area and the base is pretty good, you are already there before everything goes to pieces. I make sure they are ready before I take them out.

How do you go about lengthening and shaping the outrun?

Stretch them out and if they are not right, stop them and get in their eye a little bit, and put that pressure on that they understand because you started it at hand—you can step in and they will turn off and give to you. I should be able to get a dog to give to me stepping in to him from 100 yards away, walking toward him a little bit, and as soon as he flares and gives off me then I go the other way, take that pressure off and let him be correct. I'm not chasing him around on the outrun— pushing, pushing, keeping that pressure on. When the dog flares out and gives, I take the pressure off. If he is not correct, I stop him again. But I don't stretch them out to 800 yards right away, I graduate it up and if they are right I proceed as the dog is ready.

How do you start them on driving?

They know a "there" in the small area. I've got them stopping at any point around the clock and walking into the sheep, "Right there, walk, walk." I walk them right into the sheep until the sheep turn and move off me. I'll walk beside them and encourage them, and it is not unfamiliar when you step out and you are in a bigger area. I think a mistake a lot of new handlers make is wearing sheep too much. These dogs know how to wear sheep. Border collies go to balance; they know that. That unfamiliar thing is to have the dog on the same side as you, or parallel to you, or something like that. So I introduce it right away. Most of them take to driving pretty easily. They might not hook on to it right away and go, but they understand that being on the same side as me is not an unfamiliar thing. And I can get behind a bigger group of sheep— I have the luxury of having work to do—and a lot of my dogs will be great driving dogs on a big flock right away. You get behind them and it's "hey" to correct and get them to come back behind. Keying down to three is what takes time, but they get it.

What are some common problems that you see when you start young dogs, and how do you address those problems? For example, if you see a dog that is too wide, how would you address that?

There are all the tricks and you talk to people that have had those problems. I've had a wide dog and it was a big issue and I wouldn't want another one. A lot of stuff is obedience—for example, a dog that is really, really sticky and has too much eye. Basically, if you say "come-bye," it should mean "come-bye," not just twitch his head in that direction and stick. He should move. I want a dog that can go to a trial and also get a day's work done. A gripper and a biter, why is he doing it, is it tension? Is it just a habit he's gotten into somewhere else? If it were one of mine, I'm going to work it out pretty early. If he won't stop well I back it up and get back into a small area. Things that are inherent in the dog, like too much eye or too wide, if it's a fault that you can live with you proceed, and if is one you can't live with, you don't. If it's a really weak dog that won't face sheep because it is a bit of a coward, it goes; I wouldn't deal with it. A lot of us do, especially with our first dog, or the ones that we just love, or because of genetics, ("I've got to have a son of good old Kep"), and we keep it no matter what. I've learned to be less sentimental about it. I had a really special dog called Decks, and I never got a pup or even a grandpup from him, and I'm not going to get one. But I've tried a few, kept them longer than I should have. You've got to be able to be critical. Every dog has faults, they've all got a hole somewhere. But if you can live with it, and be sort of good-humored about it, great. Figure out what the holes are and then see if you can live with them, and if you can't they should go to someone else. They might suit somebody else.

Do you want to talk a bit about how you introduce the shed and how that process goes?

Just work a bigger group of sheep, make a hole and ask the pup through. When the situation presents itself, make the situation. Just get them so that they will come to you through a group of sheep right away early on. When I start picking up on him, he's got that base on him, he's obedient, and I can control him. I'll be out doing a job and maybe I do have to shed off a group and take them somewhere. Ask that pup to come through the middle a little bit. It is an easy ask, not a situation where he is going to fail. Not hair sheep that are splitting and diving behind me. But just a big group and you can make a hole with the other dog or make a hole yourself right through there, and get that pup to come through and take those sheep away, so it starts to become just another familiar thing, so that having sheep on both sides isn't something unusual. Some of them take to it right away, and for others it is a bit more of an ask and you have to make a huge hole and praise them a lot. It is the novice handler mistake that you get this dog moving up through the classes and he's five and you're never going to be able to run him in Open because he's never shed. It is such a foreign thing that it becomes a difficult thing to teach them. I think the more you can introduce them to early on, the better off you are going to be at the end.

When do you introduce whistles?

Usually I'll start with a stop whistle and walk-up whistle even in the pen. Just a little bit right away. They've got a recall already because they are part of a pack. As soon as I start taking them out and doing some gathering they are picking up on the whistles, and I do a bit of schooling so they are getting those whistles. I'm schooling even when I'm working, I'm just really training all of the time. If he's wrong, I try to make him right. I take the time to make the habits ingrained, with the dog working the way I want him to.

Do you use the same whistles for all of your dogs?

At the moment I do. I'm not linguistically very gifted, and I do give wrong flanks a lot.

When do you like to start entering your dogs in trials? What do you like to get out of early trials?

It really depends on the dog. I'm not an advocate of having these ten-month-old puppies out there running in Nursery. If I have a precocious young one that's ready, I may enter, but I'm always ready to leave the post if things go wrong. The trials are too expensive to go if the dogs are not prepared. They've got to be driving, they've got to be running well. Here in the East, we have some trials with pretty short outruns, they can be good for getting pups used to trials, but sometimes the sheep are kind of bad. So, it really depends on the dog and where I am in the country. I wouldn't be throwing my dog out there at Meeker for his first trial. But if I had an opportunity to get to the post with the young dog a little bit and I thought he was prepared, I'd do it.

Do you put thought into choosing particular trials for your dogs, or do you just enter your dogs when you think they are ready?

What I see at trials, especially at trials here in the northeast, is a lot of dogs running at the pro-novice level who are not prepared. They are splitting sheep at the top and chasing them down the field, they aren't covering, and they have no off-balance flanks on the fetch. To my mind, I don't want to be spending my thirty dollars to chase sheep around the field. My dog better stop, it better have an off-balance flank, it better have an inside flank on a cross drive before I am going to take him to the post. It doesn't do the pup any good to go out there and get away with stuff at a distance that is outside of his depth. If you want to be competitive in the Nursery, you can put an awful lot of pressure on a young dog. But saying that, I've had some that were going to the trials before they were two. Maybe they weren't completely competitive, but they were at least ready to deal with the situations; if they're not, I am very happy to leave the post before things go to pieces.

What is the most important thing that you think that people should keep in mind when they are training a dog?

Well, I guess maybe something that Bobby Henderson said that had been passed on to me: show them what you want. You know, we think we are great trainers. We all do, we get these dogs trained up, but you are not training them so much as showing them what you want. If you tried it twice and they are not getting it, change your method. Always remember that the dogs are trying their best to cue into *our* body language and *our* signals and *our* vocabulary. We can get as mad as we want, but is that going to make them try any harder? No. Also, remember that if there is a hole in a dog that you can't live with, don't stick with it to the point that you are wasting a lot of time. There are a lot of good ones out there, and there is also a good home for every dog.

Carol Campion

HAMPTON, CONNECTICUT

Carol Campion lives on a small sheep farm in northeast Connecticut with her husband Larry and numerous border collies, fifty sheep, and two cats. She has been training and trialing Border Collies since 1984. Since moving to Bittersweet Farm in 1997, she has been focusing on breeding and training which allows her to spend more time on the farm. Carol is well respected for her success in bringing along young dogs and her gift for helping others learn to train their dogs effectively.

"I find that a lot of what you can get done—impressions that you can build in a young dog—can be developed by just not allowing them to do the wrong thing."

How long have you been involved in sheepdogs? How did your involvement come about? Which came first, your sheep or your dogs?

We first got sheep probably 25 or 30 years ago. The sheep predated the dogs by quite a bit. We bought our original sheep, a flock of Romneys, for my spinning and weaving. That's what I used to do. We would go to sheep and wool festivals to sell fiber. While we were there, my husband Larry would go watch the dog trials. I had no interest in them, but he would go. Eventually, maybe 23 years ago, I went to Edgar Gould and bought Larry a border collie puppy for Christmas. And that was the beginning of it. I got him the dog and eventually tried working it myself, and one thing led to another and here we are! She was not a great dog by any means. In fact, she was a very difficult dog. Looking back on it now, I know that she was extremely loose-eyed and very bull-headed. She came from really good breeding, but she was difficult. When my daughter and I went to pick her out, she was the only one that he had left and she was hiding. We actually had to find her. But none of the little red flags went up, so we brought her home. She was afraid of people. She wasn't socialized. But we trained her, and Larry and I both ran her. She was my first novice dog. In fact there are some old NEBCA Newsletter issues or *Working Border Collie* issues with my name in there running her in novice back at Steve Wetmore's trial. To her credit, she had incredible stamina and she had lots of courage and determination. She was good at moving sheep, but she was quite loose-eyed and didn't want to listen. She was just a tough first dog.

Do you take in dogs for training?

Yes.

How many dogs do you start a year on average?

Well, I usually have going maybe three or four young ones of my own that I'm starting. In the summer months, or when the weather is mild, I'll have fifteen to twenty people a week that come for lessons. A lot of those people are coming with brand new dogs and end up trialing with them, so I basically feel like I've started those dogs. In some cases I do, because some of the people don't want to work them at all until they get going. Usually I have four or five outside dogs in for training at a time. In the summer, when people are coming for lessons, they're here in the morning, and in the afternoon it's too hot to train, and then in the evening I take my own dogs out. So, in the summer I usually have less time for outside dogs than in the winter. The winter is a good time to take in dogs, but then you deal with whether there is snow or not.

What do you consider the ideal age for starting a dog?

I think that it is best to start them when they are at least a year old. I don't think that they shouldn't see sheep, or not be near them until then, but I don't think it gives you any benefit to starting serious pressure kind of training before a year because a lot of times they are not ready to take it. I find it is like people who send their kids to preschool and want them learning to read and stuff before they start school. The kids that have been held back to the normal time and start school at the usual age of five or so catch up to any early learners anyway, and they haven't gone through the stress of being made to do it too early. I think young dogs are the same. What I find is that I'll take my puppies out at eight or nine weeks of age to see the sheep, and again at intervals every couple of weeks just so they get to see the sheep moving and are introduced to the smell of them. I like seeing their instincts kick in, seeing them wanting to work. What I have found is that if you take a pup at five months that is from good breeding, keen to work, and you take it to sheep, a lot of times you'll see them cast out or show you some spark of brilliance that just takes your breath away. But generally I find that when you take those same puppies out again at seven or eight months they can be little hellions. Then if you wait and take them out again at about a year, they are back to looking more like that dog you saw at five months, or somewhere in between. So a lot of that hellion stuff goes away just by itself if you wait until they are older to start them.

What specifically do you do when you take younger pups to sheep to get them accustomed to sheep before you are actually ready to start them?

Usually I introduce pups to sheep outside somewhere. I don't usually take them into a barn, or if I did I'd be holding them because there are too many places for a puppy to get hurt loose in a barn with sheep. My sheep are outside most of the time anyway. If someone is coming for a lesson and I have some sheep in a smaller area where the puppy can see sheep going by, I'll bring the pup along. I'll even let the puppy into a smaller training area—not a tiny pen by any means, but certainly something where there is room where I can make sure the puppy isn't going to get trampled or hurt. I'll put it in and just move the sheep myself or have another dog move the sheep just to let the puppy see them move, smell them, and just be around it all. I think it all registers somewhere.

On a line or loose?

It depends. A lot of times they won't appear to be paying any attention but they are still smelling the sheep or seeing them. Sometimes I'll have the pup on a very thin cord in case it does take off. Sometimes the sheep may start to come toward you, so if the pup is near you it might think the sheep are coming after him. So I'll want to be in a position to scoop it up if necessary. Mostly I just want the puppy to see sheep and smell them. Sometimes I'll use an older dog to turn them. Most of the time it's the motion of the sheep moving away that kicks in their interest. People will say, "Oh, I got a puppy and brought it to sheep and it had no interest," but the sheep will be just standing there. Pups have no interest in that. If the sheep move away, that motion will make that instinct kick in.

What do you look for in a pup? What would be the ideal pup? Are you choosing strictly by pedigree or bloodlines?

On litters that I've bred myself, I generally would take pretty much any pup in the litter unless I have a feeling about the line or there is some history there—some bloodlines throw better males than females, for instance. If I have a sense of that, then I'll factor that in. But generally if it is something I've bred, I usually let people take what they want and keep what is left. But aside from just having information about the breeding, I don't want one that is timid—I've learned that because my first border collie was a basket case—and I don't want one that is too bold and hyper. I want one that is just kind of settled and confident. One thing I do look for now is a good tail on them even from the time they are four weeks old. I look for a good tail and a dark eye. You can see that on them even then. When they come up to the feed bowl, I look for the ones that have that nice j-shaped tail, just nicely down and turned up, not a kinky tail or anything like that.

Do you find that you prefer to work dogs or bitches as a rule?

No, no difference.

How are your pups raised?

They're whelped in the house. If I want to keep more than one, I might arrange for students to take some to raise. I like keeping just one here. It is raised in the house. Sleeps in a crate. Gets housebroken. That kind of thing. I tend not to take them with me to a lot of places, not for any reason—I just don't go to that many places. Being here with me, they don't get out in cars and travel much. Letting other people take them, they tend to do that stuff with the puppy, which is good. I think it is good for the pups to have that experience, I just don't have that much opportunity to do it.

How often do you see them when they are farmed out?

Usually they are raised by students, so they bring them every couple weeks and we'll just put them on sheep to see what they are doing.

When do you like to see a pup show interest in stock? When would you start to get nervous if it weren't showing an interest?

I *like* them to show interest at nine weeks old. If I had a dog that I bred who really wasn't showing any interest by the time it was eight or nine months, I'd start thinking about moving it along. Definitely by the time it was a year, if it wasn't showing interest I'd move it along. It could be a late bloomer, but I just don't want to wait that long. If I had a dog that I brought out on sheep and I could see it was really afraid of them, I'd move it along. I've had people come out with extremely well-bred border collies that were terrified of the sheep. Some of them get over it, but a lot of them never completely do, and I definitely wouldn't want to keep one of those.

How old are they when you start formal training?

Nine months to a year.

What would you consider to be too old to be worth the time and effort it takes to train a dog?

I don't consider that there is an age that makes one too old, but it depends on what the dog has been doing in that time. If you have a talented dog from really good breeding that has been getting away with murder for three years of its life, running the show, regardless of how talented it is, you're going to have a hard time getting into its head. It really depends on how it is raised and what kinds of things have happened to it in that period of time. Otherwise, I've had dogs here that were three or four, and they've turned on and learned incredibly fast just right away. I've heard people say that there is a window of opportunity between a year and a year and a half, and, yeah, sure they are ready to start training at a year, and by a year and a half you can have a lot done with them, but I've had dogs that are two or three years old that have done fine. What happens with some people who have been doing sports like agility is that the dogs are reading a body language there that is almost opposite of what you want for having a dog work livestock, and you end up with real conflicts. So you can find that some of them have spent too many years doing something else that makes training them difficult, as opposed to its being strictly about the dog's age.

What sort of sheep do you like to start pups on? How many sheep would you typically use?

I have Border Leicester/Cheviot crosses, and I also have purebred Katahdin sheep. Every year I'll hold back maybe a dozen lambs, and when late summer comes I'll break them with the dogs and then use them as my training sheep for the winter. So I start my dogs on fairly well-broke, not sour, sheep that are used to seeing a dog, that aren't going to challenge a dog, and that are going to move respectfully off a dog, making it rewarding for the dog to work them. It is usually a mix, there are usually some Border Leicester/Cheviots and some Katahdins. And sometimes, with each batch, I can get three or four Katahdins out of that bunch that are really perfect for young dogs, just perfect. They don't panic and try to run off, they just move off nicely, and they don't bump into people. When I find them, I'll make a note of which ones they are. Then when someone is coming or I'm taking a puppy out, I'll just shed those out and work those, so they stay really broke for young dogs. They get so used to seeing everything, that stuff doesn't ruffle them. They know the program, they're not so broke that they're sour, yet they're not overly reactive. So they make it so that the dog can focus on what it is doing, rather than worrying about the sheep taking off.

Do you ever introduce your pups to something other than sheep, say ducks or goats?

No. Let me just mention my little experience with goats. I've only been around one flock of Boer goats; I watched them being worked, and I've worked some dogs on them myself. I felt that they were almost too heavy and too non-reactive, so much so that some younger dogs didn't turn on because the goats weren't moving enough. Also, the goats needed a push that some young dogs weren't ready to do. I know a lot of people do use them, but I didn't care for them in my experience. But it is a limited experience.

What size field do you prefer for starting a pup? Do you ever make use of a round pen?

I usually start them in an enclosed area that is probably about fifty to sixty by eighty to ninety feet. It is an oval-shaped area. I usually start them in there, not because the dogs need it but because the sheep need it. When you walk onto a field with a dog that is untrained, the sheep can feel it, and if they can take off, they will. Even though I have fifty acres here, if I walk out to my field with a dog that is not trained and the sheep see it coming, they'll take off. So that is already a strike against the young dog that I'm trying to start. At this farm, it has to do with how much pressure I have on my field toward buildings, gates, etc. If it were a big, huge, open field with no draw toward anything, it wouldn't matter because the sheep would be content to stay in the middle. But my sheep are always trying to get somewhere with a dog that they don't know, so I generally start in an enclosed area so they don't get in the habit of taking off.

So, you'd be introducing dogs in the enclosure with the whole dozen of the lambs you've set aside for training?

It might be, or it might be just four or five of them. Usually it's about half of the dozen, because I don't know what these dogs are going to be like. If you get one that is the fly-into-the-middle type of dog, then it can get to be chaos. So, usually I start with five or six sheep, sometimes even eight.

Are there any aids that you make use of as a general rule, say a whip or a pvc pole?

Generally, my favorite tool is a very thin long line. I find that a lot of what you can get done—impressions that you can build in a young dog—can be developed by just not allowing them to do the wrong thing. If you have a long line, you can prevent them from doing the wrong thing when they don't know a stop and when they don't know any commands. Then I have a small buggy whip, actually more of a dressage whip, that I can hit against my boot or my leg to make a noise. I can use my hand or my hat or anything to turn the dog's head out, but my long line is really my favorite thing.

How long would you stay in the enclosure? Obviously it depends on the dog and how it is coming along, but as a general rule?

My enclosure is big enough that I can actually stay in there as long as I need. My goal is not "to teach an outrun" in there; my goal is to teach the pup how to cast around sheep properly, how to hold an arc and not cut in when casting around sheep, how to stop, how to walk up, how to drive the sheep away from me. All of those things I do up close. So really I don't need a big space to do it. That training pen is within a field that is probably two to three acres, and I will stay in that training pen as a rule of thumb until the dog is casting properly around without cutting in, when it will flank without cutting in, when it will stop wherever I tell it on balance and off balance, and when it is starting to learn its flanks and when it will come off the sheep willingly without me dragging it off. Then, I feel like I can take it out into the field. What I do is I make sure that those same sheep that I've been working in the pen are the sheep that go outside into the field; I'll use those same sheep that I used in the enclosure because they already know the dog and they are not going to panic. Once the dog has the ability to bend properly around the sheep without cutting in, it is not going to unnerve the sheep or panic them. So, once you've got all that stuff done, going from the pen out to the field is a really easy transition; everything is the same. The dog already knows what is expected of him. It is the same thing they've done in the pen.

So you generally don't enlist the aid of a fully-trained dog when you're working a young dog in a larger field for the first few times?

No, I never use an older dog anymore for training a young dog. I don't have to.

What do you like to see in a pup's first few sessions? What would tell you that the pup might be a good prospect?

For me, I like a dog that shows a method, that has some sense of trying to feel where to be on its sheep. I like to see a dog that is responsive to me and where I am, without too much pressure put on it. Everybody likes a dog that just casts right around its sheep—of course, that's great—and one that holds a nice distance once it gets there and brings its sheep to you. Really, I would love to see that. But usually the first couple of times you bring them out, they don't even see you, it's just them and the sheep. So the first time can be kind of rough. I like a dog that by the end of the first session is casting around its sheep and giving them some room while paying attention to me, showing that it is responsible but has some method with the stock. That's what I'm looking for.

What would be a big red flag? What might warn you of later problems?

A dog that is terrified of sheep. What you'll see in those dogs is that they are the ones that will be wanting to grip. In a lot of cases, dogs that are terrified of sheep are either not going to want to come onto their sheep, not going to want to walk up, and if they do come on they may be tearing into them. That kind of thing. You can get puppies or young dogs that are gripping or rough for other reasons, and a lot of those things can be worked through pretty easily. But in dogs that are afraid of the sheep or have a lack of confidence that is based on a real fear and not just a lack of experience, that fear brings out some behaviors that are going to be hard to change.

How do you handle pups that want to grip?

Usually if I get a pup that is seven or eight months old that is gripping, I'll try putting a little pressure on it, maybe catch it on a line and give it a gruff voice or something. It depends how old they are. If they are young, I won't put on tons of pressure, I'll assume that it is just immaturity and I'll put it up. I've had dogs that I've put up for a month or two that just stop doing it.

So you would never just ignore it on the assumption that the behavior will extinguish itself in time?

No, because I believe that the sheep need to be protected and the sheep don't like being chewed up for the sake of the dog trying to train itself. Generally, I don't even correct the pup; I have it on a line, and I've been doing it long enough so that I'm catching it before it grips. Maybe sometimes they'll have gotten away with it once, but usually you can see it coming and stop them before they get to that point. Then, if you can make a noise or something just before the point that the dog is going to grip, it will often deter it so that it will look for something else to do there like bend out. If that sort of thing doesn't work on a dog that is seven, eight, or nine months old, I'll try putting it up for a month or so, because in some cases it is just nervousness and it will go away on its own.

What would you say about some mild avoidance when a pup is first introduced to sheep, like sniffing or acting like the sheep aren't there?

I've had some people come and have dogs do that for like ten minutes and then, if you just keep moving the sheep around, all of a sudden it's like someone turned the switch on; the pup becomes interested and intense. So that doesn't bother me that much. If I have one that stays that way for fifteen or twenty minutes and goes home like that, that doesn't bother me that much. If it continued, if it came back a couple of times and still did that as it got older and was around the sheep more, that *would* bother me. But a lot of times they'll start out that way, and then all of a sudden, it's like someone lifted a blind or something: they'll cast out or flank around and then you can't get their attention *off* the sheep. I don't know what it is; it's a pretty amazing thing.

Is there anything you want them to know before they are introduced to sheep?

It's not required, but I think it's kind of nice if they know what the words "lie down" mean before they first go to sheep. One thing I do really want, and I've told this to the people that leave their dogs here, is that they need to know how to walk on a line or a lead. You'd be surprised how many dogs can't do that. The reason is, a lot of people raise their dogs in an environment where they don't ever need one. If their dogs are just in the yard or around the house, they never need to put them on a lead. But I'll put them on a line and they just drag me, especially once they start getting used to going out to sheep. So I like a dog to know how to walk on a line and at least to acknowledge when it hears its name.

Is there a dog of your own that stands out in your mind as one that showed a lot of promise when it was first started? How did that dog turn out? Have you found the ones that are easiest to train are usually the ones that turn out the best, or is there not necessarily any link?

There is definitely a link because I think you can see good breeding coming through. Though I've had some extremely well-bred dogs here that I found to be really worthless and useless. One dog of my own that I have now that has been pretty rewarding to work with is Evie. From the time she was ten weeks old, you could put her down in front of a group of sheep, and she was that dog I'm talking about that would just cast around and bring them to you. She'd bring them, get them to you, and lie down on her own.

So the special ones kind of stand out?

Yes, but I've had dogs that started that way that didn't amount to anything. Because they will somewhere get to a point where something is required of them and they just don't have it. It may be something in their nature in terms of trainability or whatever. It sure is a pleasure to get one that has it the whole way.

How about just the opposite, have you ever had one that you thought was not good at all initially that turned out well in the end?

Yeah. I have one that has just started to run in Open for me. She was one that had a bit of a heading instinct, so that she'd start around sheep and as soon as sheep would turn and come towards her, she'd cut in front of them, then shoulder them and try to grab them. She kind of outgrew that by herself, but she wasn't really ready to train until she was between a year and a year and a half old. I took her to sheep quite a bit, but she was trying to grab them on her way around. So I didn't do a lot of training because if I did, I would have had to do something about that. So I kind of left her alone, and when I took her out I'd make sure that sheep were moving away from her when I'd send her. When she reached a year or a little over a year, all of that left on its own and then she trained up incredibly fast.

How and when do you introduce a stop?

I usually try to get the dog at least to acknowledge that I want them to stop by allowing the dog to get to balance, taking the sheep to a fence, then blocking the dog until it comes to a stop, and then I'll tell them to stop. Even if the dog already knows a lie down or a stop off of sheep, when you get them to sheep for some of them it has absolutely no relevance. They don't make any connection. So to stand there yelling "lie down" is not a good thing because to the dog it's not the same thing. I'll wait until they are stopped and then say "lie down," or I'll wait until they are stopped then walk towards them, pick up the line, and say "that'll do." I try to build on that. I do it really early on, because I use stopping a lot. I find that it is a good way to keep the dog from doing stuff that is wrong.

So you like to introduce commands by repeating the word several times when the dog is doing the behavior?

I do like to get a behavior and then add the word to it. But I've learned to make sure that they are doing it *properly* before I put a word on it. If they are just going in a direction aiming toward the sheep, you are just going to associate the word with a lousy flank and have to go and fix it later. I'll introduce my flanks without saying anything, just using body language to make sure that they turn out when they flank and are doing it properly. I like them to hear it just after they've started taking it. You can see it in their face when they are choosing to do it. I think that is when they are open to hearing it and associating the word with the behavior.

When, if ever, do you start to insist on absolute obedience to your commands? How do you balance obedience with developing the pup's initiative and confidence and that sort of thing?

I'm of the belief that if you ask them to do something they have to do it, otherwise they never learn what the words mean. So I wait until I have them doing the behavior, and then I put the command on it. I'll do that for a little while and then when I know that the dog knows what I mean, I'll start asking them to be obedient. Then, once I've said it, I want them to do it so it becomes second nature to give me what I ask. If you mix that together with allowing the dog to work and be natural when you give them their sheep, then you get both a dog that can work and feel its sheep in addition to a dog that can be obedient. When they are bringing the sheep to me on balance, I might just say "there now" or "steady" or maybe say nothing, and I'll let them just work. I make sure that along with asking for obedience and teaching them flanks and teaching them to stop and teaching them to come off balance, I'll also allow them to get to balance often enough and just bring me the sheep, and I'll alter things and change situations so that they are learning to read sheep and feel them because they need that as well.

How soon do you introduce the drive? Do you want them to have a certain length of outrun first before teaching the drive?

No, I don't wait for a certain length outrun. I do it all fairly early on. As I said, I don't "teach an outrun." I teach them how to cast properly around their sheep. Dogs that have a method and a good sense of balance are going to go to balance and bring you the sheep. But I don't build a dog's training on always being at twelve o'clock. Pretty early on in a dog's training, I'm teaching them to come off balance and flank off balance, and at the same time I'm also introducing stopping anywhere both on and off balance. Once they'll flank off balance and stop anywhere, then I start asking them to walk up at any point and just take the sheep. Initially, I'm just asking them to walk up and just make enough contact so that they can feel they've made contact. Gradually I add letting them just take the sheep. You can get a sense of when a dog is ready to do it. Some young dogs go nicely around the sheep, stop, bring them to me, and get them a certain distance from me and just lie down and not come any closer. I remember with Eve thinking "here's a dog that's afraid to get close to her sheep." And all of a sudden, one day the sheep just turned around, because often once you stop the dog the sheep will turn around to see where the dog is, and she just got up and kept on coming and from that point she started driving. Because she decided she wanted to move them. So they all have a different time schedule for when they are really ready to take sheep and drive them. But I introduce coming off balance and walking up on the sheep from different points pretty early on as groundwork for the drive.

Do you use any flank commands on those early drives? Are you particular about where they are driving the sheep, or do you hold off until they are pushing them fairly confidently?

No, usually I just want them to get a feel for being on the pressure and holding the line. I don't care where they take them. I'll let them go and if it looks like they are going to veer around the sheep and come off the pressure, I'll stop them. But I try not to use flanks yet. I want my flanks in a young dog to be something separate. I'm trying to teach them so that they learn them as a tool rather than teaching a drive based on flanking. I want them just to take the sheep, just the same as on a fetch. I want them to feel where they need to be to control the sheep and just take them. Once they have a sense of holding a line, then I'll introducing flanks, not to steer the sheep but to show the dog how to give up control of the sheep to be repositioned, when necessary.

When do you introduce whistles? Do you start with a single whistle, say just the stop whistle?

I usually get them on voice commands first and then add whistles. I start with the stop whistle, or maybe the stop and the walk up. I usually say the word, then blow the whistle, then gradually shift it until I can just blow the whistle and not say anything at all.

Same whistles for all of your dogs?

Yes.

When do you introduce shedding? What is your approach?

Fairly early, but in order to do it you need a dog that is under some control. You have to be able to steady them up in a position in order to cause the sheep to split. Maybe between a year and a year and a half if they'll do it. I don't force it, but if the opportunity is there I'll do it just so the dog gets comfortable with it. I used to wait until they had the dog trial sequence of behaviors down, but I realized that can be detrimental to the training of border collies. It seems logical to assume that the dog can't go to college until it's finished kindergarten, but with border collies it just doesn't work that way. They can do all of it. In fact, some dogs learn to drive better by shedding and having something to push away from something else. If I have a dog that is steadying up and is biddable, and I can flank it and stop it in a position to cause the sheep to split, I'll start calling the dog to me. If the sheep are spread out and it is easy to keep them apart without a fight, I might call them to me and wear a group away, it just depends on the situation.

Do you introduce the look back with the shed?

If there is an opportunity, I'll introduce it. Some dogs get the idea really easily, while others are just really clueless as to what you are talking about because they just can't get their eyes off of the sheep in front of them. Shedding for some really is the best place to do it. If I'm working a group of sheep and there is another group of sheep off in the distance that the dog doesn't know is there, I'll use that opportunity to teach look, or look for your sheep. Really, though, I think that shedding is the easiest time to do that.

Do you think a dog needs to be taught a grip at some point so that it can defend itself?

I think it depends on the dog. I think there is a tendency for people to try to teach their dog to stay off the stock because the dog that is far away settles the sheep and often tends to be the dog that does better at the Saturday dog trial. But in doing that, a lot of times dogs are led to believe that staying off the sheep is the only thing that they should do. I think that rather than focusing on just teaching a grip, you should teach a dog how to come on to its sheep at the same time that you are teaching the dog how to back off its sheep. Teach the dog how to get on to the pressure and come forward, and when to do it. In some cases, what you are looking for is for the dog to come forward and not necessarily to bite the sheep, but just to come forward. There are cases where if the dog grips, the sheep are not going to turn and move away, whereas if that dog would just come forward a few steps, the sheep would turn away. So I think it is more of a case of teaching a dog to come on to its sheep, and not just get off of its sheep. It is nice to have a dog that will grip, and if I've got sheep coming after my dog I surely want him to grip them, I don't want the dog to think that he isn't allowed to. I think lots of dogs really think that they are not supposed to get near the sheep and that has to do with how they are trained. So, no, I am not opposed to teaching the grip at all, but I do think that the first thing that I would want to do is to teach a dog how to come forward.

What about trialing? How soon in a dog's training do you start to enter trials? Do you want them to be pretty polished and ready first, or do you enter trials to get your dog experience on other fields along the way?

I generally wait until they are at least trained to do the work well beyond the class that I'm entering them in. I want it to be easy for them when they get to a trial. I don't go to a lot of other places, I generally just work here, so my dogs often enter a trial without having worked anywhere but here. I don't believe that you can train them on the trial field. I think they learn from repetition and they can learn to do things wrong as well as right.

How about the Nursery program? Do you generally like to participate in trialing in Nursery? Do you think it is detrimental to dogs to be pushing them to get ready for Nursery?

I don't think it is necessarily detrimental. Of all the dogs that I've had here, there have only been one or two that I would not have been pushing to run in Nursery. I *have* found myself having a dog that is just about ready to run really successfully in Pro-Novice but maybe its outrun is just a little tight, or something is not quite a hundred percent for me, but if a trial is coming up and I've entered it I'll find myself really putting pressure on the dog to get off the sheep and stuff, and then I'll realize I wouldn't be putting that pressure on the dog if it weren't for the dog trial. So I tend to wait until they are really ready to run until I run them.

Would you be happy with a dog that was strictly a trial dog but not a useful farm dog?

I think that any dog that I owned to be a trial dog could be a useful farm dogs just because of the way that I train. I don't train them just to do outrun, lift, and fetch; I train them to learn how to cast around sheep and how to gain proper control of sheep with a decent cast, walking forward when it is time to walk forward and staying on the pressure and getting ahold of their sheep.

Since you've been involved in sheepdog training and trialing for some eighteen years now, how have you seen the dogs

changing, if at all? Is there a trend in the way things are go-
ing? Are dogs getting more talented, less talented? Are we
selecting for weaker trial dogs?

I think the general level of quality of these dogs is quite a bit
higher than it was when I first got dogs. Definitely. You are
always going to find weak dogs and tough dogs and that kind
of thing, because certain types of dogs suit certain people. I
think that a lot of people that trial don't have the kind of work
that allows them to see whether their dog is light or not, there
is just no way they would ever know, no conditions to find
out, really. But I think that the quality of dogs is definitely
way up there. You can have a dog that is a little light that can
still be a top quality dog. A lot of times the sheep like that
kind of dog, and they'll move off of them more readily than
they will a stronger dog. It depends on how they are trained
and handled, but the quality of dogs has definitely improved.
I think you see dogs over here that are as nice, if not better,
than the dogs that you see overseas. I've been over many,
many times now, seeing a lot of dogs, and I really believe
that.

What is the most important tip that you would like to pass
along to others that are interested in training a puppy?

Look at each dog as an individual and do not assume that if
your dog is not doing it right he is being disobedient or bad.
Look at training as a way to teach dogs how to manage livestock in a partnership rather than to get an animal ready for a
dog trial. I think you get a more well-rounded type of a dog
that way. Training dogs just for a dog trial tends to short-
change some of the training that you can do with them.

SCOTT GLEN

ALBERTA, CANADA

Scott Glen has been training and trialing border collies to herd sheep and cattle for over twenty years. As successful a dog breeder as he is a trainer and handler, Scott is one of the few to have competed successfully with over four generations of the same homebred line, all stemming from his foundation sire Sweep. It was, in fact, Sweep's grandson Pleat who became the 2004 USBCHA/ABCA champion, making Scott the first Canadian to win the title.

"I'm really trying to develop a dog that's a little bit pushy, and then back him off later."

How many dogs do you start a year?

Fifteen. The majority are client dogs, but some are mine.

When you're picking a pup for yourself, what do you look for?

Something that attracts me, that catches my eye—it might not be anything that I can describe easily. Sometimes a puppy will just jump out at you as the one. Other times I pick one that I like the look of. I like pups to be nicely marked, without too much white. But sometimes a pup will jump out at you that isn't at all what you'd expect to like physically.

Do you prefer males or females?

It doesn't really matter to me. I have more males than females, but it's not by design; it just happens to be the way it goes.

How do you raise your puppies?

They're in a kennel. When they're little, I spend quite a bit of time with them in the evenings and mornings. I don't like letting them run together—once they're weaned I like to get them off by themselves. I don't like keeping more than one out of a litter whenever possible.

When do you like your pups to show an initial interest in sheep?

It doesn't matter at all. I've seen dogs wanting to work sheep at a couple of months old. Some turn out well, and some really never *do* turn out well, other than the fact that they always want to work. But as far as real quality dogs, I've seen real good ones show an interest at three months, and I've seen real good ones turning on as late as ten or eleven months. It's nice when they start early, because at least you know they're interested.

Do you let pups follow you around while you're doing chores, before you start training them?

No, I don't let them follow me, once they're interested; I don't take them to sheep until I'm really ready to start them, at around ten or eleven months. With my schedule, I'm usually doing work with the stock while I'm walking around. If the pups aren't interested yet, the chances of them getting hurt are too great. And if they're interested, the chances of things going wrong is a problem. So I'll have a dog or two with me who are already going well, but not a puppy.

How old are your pups when you start formal training?

Eight to twelve months. I like them to have a lie down before I start them on stock.

So you teach them a lie down away from stock?

Yes. I've done it both ways, but it's just easier on me and on the sheep when they know it before we start.

Do you want them to know anything else?

I also like them to know a "that'll do" command. And it's important that they have a relationship with me before we start training. Even with client dogs, I don't start them the very day that they come in. I spend some time with them, teaching them a lie down off the stock, just so we'll get some rapport going. If they're a little bit cautious, I won't start training them until they bond with me a little and start trusting me. If they start getting into the sheep and they don't know me, I don't want them to be afraid of me.

What does your first training session look like? How many sheep do you use initially? What size field do you prefer?

I start with a round pen (or any small, enclosed area) quite a bit, so the dog can't get out and I can keep things from getting too wild. (It'll get wild enough from time to time anyway!) I like to use enough sheep to keep the sheep from panicking, but if I use too many I can't get to the dog to help if he needs it. That usually means that I end up using about five or six fairly calm sheep. I like the sheep to be sensible: they don't have to be entirely dogged (when I start pups in the summer, they haven't seen dogs for awhile and have freshened up because of it), but I don't want anything highheaded that will end up slamming into the fence and panicking, and I certainly don't want to use anything that seems as if it might want to take a run at the young one.

How long are they usually in the small area?

That depends. Anywhere from a couple of sessions to maybe two weeks; it just depends on how well they do. Before I take them out I want them to stop reasonably well, both on stock and off stock (once they've been introduced to stock, you might wonder where the lie down that they used to know went!). I also want to be able to recall them off the stock.

What size field do you like to use after the round pen?

It doesn't really matter—I train on sixty-five acres, but it might as well be sixty-five hundred acres; it shouldn't matter to the pup.

Do you use a trained dog to help you at this stage?

No. I'll have one around in case the sheep get away, because I don't want the pup to feel that they can just run and chase them, although of course once in awhile that happens. But I want the pup to use its initiative to try hard to stop the sheep. A lot of us have had really good first dogs that we've had a great rapport with, dogs that seemed to be able to do anything, and in my opinion the reason they seemed to be able to work like that is because those dogs have *had* to do it. If we lost the sheep, we'd have to walk back to the barn and try to figure out how to get those sheep back with the dog that we were training. If it's possible for a young dog to do a chore, I like to have it try, within reason. Those sorts of challenges that crop up can make interesting training opportunities: sometimes I might be planning to work on one thing, and I end up working on something entirely different because of opportunities that present themselves.

What do you like to see in a dog's first few sessions?

I don't like to see a dog that just refuses to use its head, that goes straight at the sheep whenever it has the chance—that's the sort of thing that might mean trouble later on. That sort of thing can be improved and maybe even fixed totally, but it's nice if they actually want to do it at least semi-right from the beginning, if they want to get around the sheep instead of just lining them up and chasing them off. I don't particularly like to see that, but having said that, if they're just excited it might not end up being anything that we have to worry about in the end, but it'll be something that we'll have to sort through. What I do like to see is a pup that casts a little bit—I don't expect them to be wide at first, but I like to see them trying to get the sheep to me as best they can. If the sheep start breaking a little bit, maybe going back to the barn, I like the pup to show an intelligent, talented way of getting around the sheep to bring them back to me. In some cases, that might mean that they're going into the middle of the group of sheep somewhat, but I like it if they're trying to use their heads to get around to the back of the sheep.

What do you do with pups who want to grip?

It depends on why they want to do it: are they doing it because they're afraid of sheep, or are they just being nasty? If they're just being a little bit nasty I'll try pretty hard not to let them by stopping them and scolding them a bit. I'd try to avoid it at first. If they're stopping well, they can't bite, unless you stop them too late. But it's a touchy thing—you want to make certain that you've evaluated it accurately at first. If they're gripping because they're afraid of sheep, it's best to wean them off of it a little bit later in order to build their confidence

What do you think are the easiest dogs to train? What are the most difficult?

The easiest dogs to train are the ones who want to cast around their sheep. That doesn't necessarily mean that at the end of the day they're going to be the best dogs, but they're certainly the easiest ones to start. Quite often those dogs are a little on the softer side—they want to stay back a little bit, and they might learn their sides a little faster. Because they can keep back, they have a good perspective on the sheep, rather than ones who are right on top of them. Those dogs can end up as really good dogs, but it won't necessarily happen that way—sometimes they're just a little bit too cautious, a little bit more followers than doers. The hardest dogs to train are often the ones that have been started wrong. Those kind of dogs might have it in their heads that they can run and just try to beat you, rather than trying to play the game: if you ask them to get out, they'll just try to run faster instead of getting out. The hardest kind of pup to train who hasn't yet been started would probably just be a stubborn one who's always into the sheep or who refuses to lie down. There's a fine line between getting the dog to stay out of the sheep and getting that dog to be as good as he can be. Anyone can get a dog to stay out of the sheep, but you need to get through to them that they're being told that they're not wrong for wanting to work the sheep, but it's just that they're working the sheep wrong.

What's the easiest dog that you've personally trained?

My Nap, whom I ran in the Nurseries, and then was run by Beverly Lambert and is now owned by Sue Schoen. That dog definitely fulfilled his early promise—he won some big Open trials by the time he was two and a half years old.

Were there some dogs that you've trained that seemed easy but who didn't go on to fulfill that early promise?

Nothing that really comes to mind, but I'm sure there have been some—there are always dogs that you're really high on that just don't have it in the end. The opposite of that is some dogs that you might not be keen on, but then all of a sudden something catches your eye and they just start developing at three or four years old.

What's your basic training process? What do you like to see a dog master before moving on to the next step?

I'm sort of picky about the gather: it doesn't have to be far, but I don't like to see them stopping short or not going around with purpose to bring the sheep back to me. I want them knowing that twelve o'clock is where they really want to be.

How do you go about showing them that?

If they start going short, I'll just try to use the pull of the sheep so that it's wrong to pull short. I'd never send them so they'd see the heads first. I'd send them to sheep that are always drifting the other way.

How do you go about lengthening the outrun?

I pay quite a bit of attention to the dog's attitude on the out-run, to figure out if they're trying to cast out a little bit wider on their own, or if they're trying to cut in every chance they get. If they're trying to cut in every time I won't try to leng-then the outrun for awhile. But sooner or later if I don't let them cut in I'll stop them and walk out and push them out, some quicker than others. You'll see those dogs start to cut in and then catch themselves a little and give ground, and that's when I'll start to introduce the length. I'm not so worried about the length from my feet—I like to lie the dog down, walk away two hundred yards, and then send it. I don't want the dog running toward me at that point and then whipping around me, the way it would do on a "that'll do"—I want to see the dog casting out.

How big an outrun do you like the dog to have mastered be-fore you start them on driving?

Probably about a hundred yards from my feet. If they can do a hundred yards from your feet it's only a matter of experi-ence before they'll do much more than that. I also like to have the dog taking a slight bit of an off-balance flank on the fetch before I start the drive.

How do you introduce driving?

I let them follow sheep—I don't expect them to push on sheep at that point; I want the sheep moving, and I just let them follow along. I don't walk behind the dog; I walk on the side. If I'm off to the dog's left or right, moving parallel, he'll be more encouraged to walk behind the sheep—it's a confidence thing. Then the dog actually starts pushing the sheep without realizing it. It's also a little easier to keep the pup from going around to the heads of the sheep if you're walking on the side.

How do you go about lengthening the drive?

I just try to wean them off needing me a little bit—one day they might be able to go twenty yards out, for instance, and I just keep encouraging them to follow behind the sheep for greater and greater distances.

When do you start insisting on absolute obedience in your commands?

With me, absolute obedience is always important with the stop—if I ask for a stop and I need it, they have to stop. I'm a little more flexible about absolute obedience on the sides—I might not start insisting on that until after the first two or three months of training. There are times that I'll let them run through the stop a little bit if they're trying to fix what they're doing wrong. I might give them a fairly hard stop because they're doing something wrong, but if they run through the stop because they're trying to fix what they've done wrong, I'll let them do that.

When do you start introducing the steady command?

Well, they'll hear the word throughout training, probably after the second month. But I won't try to get a young dog really walking unless I see that there's a particular reason I see that they're really not working well. I'm really trying to develop a dog that's a little bit pushy, and then back him off later. That's why I like to use a good stop, to keep them out of trouble, so they won't go thrashing at the sheep. I don't worry too much about pace at this stage. I'll control the pace, but if I stop the dog every time the sheep start moving too fast, the dog is going to try to avoid that a little bit. But I'm not worried about getting sheep walking at this point in training, with the dog walking nicely behind them. As long as the dog's stopping well, there's no reason the sheep should be run around too much. A stop is cut and dried to the dog; walking slowly is not. If a young dog is just trying to keep up with the sheep, trying to slow them down could confuse them. I don't want to stop a dog so much that it's always a little behind the sheep and about to lose them, but I do expect them to stop when I ask them to.

When do you introduce whistles?

My dogs hear a stop and a walkup whistle right away, almost from the very beginning. They'll probably take the whistle better on the walkup than they would on the voice. As far as flanks go, maybe three or four months; I won't bother with the whistles for the flanks until they know the voice fairly well.

How do you introduce shedding?

I just use a big group of sheep, create nice big gaps, and make sure that they have fun doing it. It depends on the dog, but I don't usually introduce shedding until the dog is running a good Nursery course. When they can do a miniature Open course like that, then I'll start introducing them to the shed.

When do you like to start entering your young dogs in trials, and what do you like to get out of those trials?

I don't like entering them until they're stopping well, and doing everything else pretty well too. I don't practice courses at home, but I'd like to know that the dog has mastered all the segments that will be encountered on a course: outruns, flanks, driving, stopping. Otherwise they'll just run through the bit, or they'll be confused and over their heads: either way, they lose.

What tip would you like to pass on to people training their first young dog?

A young dog starting out needs to enjoy himself. The biggest problem that I see with people new to trialing is trying to get a perfect trial pace too early in their young dogs. You're better off not having quite enough control early on than having too much control and taking the fun out of things for the pup. If you constantly drill your pup and make him walk, you'll take something out of him that you'll never be able to get back. There are times for working on pace and control, but it's not time when you're training up a young dog.

Bobby Henderson

HERIOT, SCOTLAND

Bobby Henderson has over thirty-five years shepherding experience and has competed at sheepdog trials for almost as long. He has won many Open trials over the years in Scotland and particularly enjoys bringing on his own young dogs through the Nursery trial leagues and onto the Open trial circuit. The highlight of his trialing career, to date, occurred in 1998 when he became the Supreme Champion at the International Sheepdog Trial, with Sweep (having been Reserve Champion two years earlier with the same dog).

"Once you're serious with training, you want the dog to do what you say. You make things easy for it at first, but you should get what you ask for."

What do you look for in a puppy?

I like a pup that's not too long and who carries his tail nicely. Usually a pup'll tell you something. You'll be looking at a litter and a pup will catch your eye. Just something about them—it's hard to put into words. I don't like them really shy, and I also don't go for the boldest one. I like a fairly short back—the short back will help the pup stand more running and be useful on the hill.

How do you raise your pups?

Normally they stay outside, but if the weather's decent we let them come into the house until they start to become a nuisance. After that they're kenneled like the rest of the dogs. We let them into the house as soon as they're taken away from the mother. I try to let the pups see the other dogs in the kennel, just for company, but they're not usually kenneled with other dogs. Seeing an older dog helps keeps them settled.

Do you let the pups follow you around while doing chores?

It's quite good if they follow you around—they learn a lot that way, like how to go through a gate and when to stay back. They're always learning, even before they actually start training.

How early do you like the pup to show an interest in sheep?

That doesn't really matter, but I would like to see something by the time they're eight months old. Sometimes it's easier if they start later, when they're not so hot. The early starters usually have more eye and are a little more fiery.

When do you start formal training?

You have to take the nature of the pup into account. If the pup is really keen and really strong-tempered, I would let them work from five or six months old with an older dog. I wouldn't really do any training—just let them watch the sheep. But I wouldn't teach them anything like their sides, even though if they happened to go left I'd tell them "come-bye" just to put a word on it. But if they were wrong, I wouldn't chase them or scold them yet. You can take them with you, but you shouldn't tear into them.

What sorts of fields do you like to use to start pups?

A flat field, not too big—you only need about an acre or so to start with, to get them solid on their sides. I don't use a round pen, although I think it could be handy and there's nothing wrong with it.

Do you use an older dog while training your pups?

Yes, I use one to keep the sheep close to me and keep the sheep together, so the pup won't chase them off. The older dog is handy, as long as it doesn't get too involved and take the pup's attention away from the sheep. You wouldn't want to use the older dog too long, just until you have some control on the pup.

How often do you train your pups?

Every three days or so when I'm starting out, and then every day or every couple of days. The training sessions are no longer than fifteen to twenty minutes, depending on what we're doing. Part of that time I just let them work the sheep, backing up and letting them bring the sheep to me. I like to keep the naturalness in the pup.

What do you like to see in a pup's first few sessions?

I like to see a decent tail; it should be down and serious. I like a pup to show some eye; if you have no eye, you have no balance. I also like to see them able to come forward on the sheep, with a little bit of power. But that's not something that all of them would have to do—I'm just talking about something that would excite me. If after a few weeks the pup doesn't want to come forward I might think there was a weakness there.

What would you think of as a serious fault that might show up early?

If the tail isn't working right, it means that the head isn't working right; I don't like to see a pup with a bad tail. I don't like to hear pups barking; it can mean they're not stable or serious.

What are your phases of training?

Once you start getting serious, you encourage the pup to take its sides, but you always should make it easy for the pup. Make the sheep move in the right direction before you ask the pup to take that flank. Keep backing up and encouraging the pup to bring you the sheep. You need some control right away to be able to keep the pup from charging into the sheep, so you start working on keeping the pup back and also a little stop. I usually get a stop on them fairly soon. I don't teach a lie down until the pup is working sheep. Until you get a stop, it's hard to teach them much. I use the "there" command, which amounts to a stop—I want them to follow the sheep around the field, and "there" means for them to turn and stop at that point, going as slowly as they can while still maintaining control. Pretty soon you'll just be able to say "there," and the pup will know to flank just the right amount to balance the sheep while bringing them to you. If you back up into a fence and have the pup bring you the sheep, you'll have more control and you'll be able to accomplish quite a bit: the pup won't be able to chase the sheep or do anything silly if your back is against a fence. The pup should ideally be flowing with the sheep and keeping a reasonable distance from them, being a bit steady, and stopping its flanks when you say "there." Then you can build on that. You can put the words "come-bye" and "away" on the flanks, and pretty soon the pup will have its sides.

And what's your next training step after that?

I try to get a better outrun, shaping it. You have to have a better outrun before you can do much. I work it at short distances and move myself to make sure the pup goes around the sheep properly. I try to encourage a pear shape if I can, but it's most important to have the pup keep the proper distance all the way around and keep the right distance as it comes behind—it's very difficult to do that and to keep control, so you're better off asking for a bit more distance on the arc. The distance behind the sheep is more important than the shape of the outrun itself.

When do you start driving?

They have to be solid on their sides before you start driving. I'd also like to have them outrunning decently. Driving is very easy to get once the dog knows its sides and will stop.

How do you start driving?

If it's an easy dog that listens well, you can start having them drive in a circle around you, flanking them back and stopping them in the right place. You need sensible sheep that are used to a dog as well. You can walk with the dog and sheep for awhile. A lot of my dogs are driving before they even realize they're doing anything unusual. If you're having trouble doing that, I'd do the exercise against the fence, walking behind them. The fence can be a big help with very strong dogs. You can walk about twenty yards away from the fence, so that even if the dog is determined to go around, you'll be in a position to stop them.

What kind of sheep do you like to use to start pups?

Fairly solid and sensible—you want the dog to be able to move the sheep, and you don't want sheep that are going to run at the dog. You want sheep that are solid but not too heavy—they need to be able to get up to move them, but they shouldn't be too heavy to lift. You want the sort of sheep that will move when the dog puts pressure on them and stop when the dog doesn't. That way they can actually learn to drive, which wouldn't be possible if the sheep just ran at the sight of the dog—running sheep teach a dog to follow, not to drive.

When do you start insisting on absolute obedience? How do you balance that with helping the dog develop confidence?

It depends on the dog. If it's a shy dog, I like to be easier on it. I like my dogs to start stopping pretty early on. Once you're serious with training, you want the dog to do what you say. You make things easy for it at first, but you should get what you ask for.

What do you do about gripping pups?

With a pup that's just starting, I let them know that I'm not happy with it, but just with a voice correction. But there again, you need the right kind of sheep. The sheep need to be close to you so you can correct if you see it happening. Timing's very important for something like that. You can usually see it coming. You want to correct it as the thought comes into their heads. If it's silly gripping, I might put a line on the pup so it can't get too far away and help it understand that it's not a good idea to do that.

How early do you introduce whistles?

The stop and the walkup whistles I introduce almost immediately. The flanking whistles I wait on until they know their sides. I like a dog that stops when it's told—I don't like a dog walking through its whistles.

What do you consider the easiest type of dog to train?

One with quite a bit of eye but not too much eye, easy-going. Not too fast in their movements—something with a sensible pace.

What would you consider one of the most difficult types of dog to train?

Something that's really pushy and plain, something that lacks eye. Without eye, the dog doesn't know where it should be. A dog with eye is trying to get where the pressure is; a dog without eye is all over the place and you'll have to pick his spot. Without eye, you need to be thinking for the dog and covering for it. The handler has to be much better with a loose-eyed dog. If a dog has eye, when the sheep move he'll move to cover it. A dog without eye will go too far and then come back too far, and that can be difficult.

When do you start introducing shedding?

They're quite well trained before I do shedding—it depends on how soon I'm needing it. If it happens to be lambing time, I'll introduce it earlier. They'll often realize that I need certain sheep and get the idea without starting formal shedding lessons. I let them take half of a large group away and then let them work them, so they realize that there's some point to shedding.

When do you like to start entering trials?

I like the dog to be pretty well trained—I don't like to enter them before they're ready. By a year and a half I'd like them to run a Nursery course. But it depends on the dog; if it's a late starter, it wouldn't be ready as quickly.

What's the most important piece of advice that you'd like to give people who are trying to train their first pup?

The most important thing is to ask for things that you're close enough to them to do something about that. You shouldn't ask them to stop if you know yourself that they're not going to be able to stop, and that you're too far away to make them stop.

David Henry

MEADOWVIEW, VIRGINIA

David Henry purchased his first border collie, Holly, in 1993, entering his first trial with her two years later. He is particularly proud of the fact that (as a novice) he trained Holly himself with great success: Holly qualified for the National Finals a staggering ten years in her long trial career, and David and Holly placed fifth in the USBHCA/ABCA National Finals in 1999. David and his wife Christine currently maintain a working sheep farm of about 150 commercial ewes.

"What I really like are the pups that are always eager to put a little bit more pressure on the stock."

Let's start with a short bio. How long have you been involved in sheepdog training and trialing? How did that involvement come about?

I got my first border collie in 1993, and that was Holly, of course. I had seen dogs work. I guess the first real working dog I saw was a border collie at a rodeo down in Tennessee. I was riding there, and I just thought it was incredible to see somebody talk to a dog, or communicate with a dog, basically like a person, and have the dog respond and go left and right and lie down when it was told.

Where did you get Holly? What was her breeding?

Her breeding was basically two farm dogs. At the time I was working at a feed store and a man came in with a border collie in the back of his truck. I told him that I'd always liked border collies, and I told him about my experience seeing one. He said, "Well, I've just bred this one. I think she's a pretty nice dog. Have you ever heard of a guy named Roy Johnson?" I said, "Yeah, he comes to County Fair and puts on a sheepdog demonstration." Holly's mother went back to his Rosco. I had seen Rosco at the County Fair and I had always enjoyed watching him—he was a great dog. I told him that I would love to have a puppy, and at the time I wanted a red dog—I just thought they were kind of unusual. They were $100 each. When Holly was three days old the breeder said, "I've got the litter here and you need to come and pick yours out." I said, "At three days old how can you pick a puppy?" He said, "There are no red ones, so you're going to have to pick a black-and-white." So I basically just picked her because she was a split-face; it just seemed like something different. Come to find out, she was the most aggressive puppy of the litter. She whipped all the males. So it was basically just luck. Luck and $100 got me started in the game.

How did you get started trialing Holly?

I took Holly to some Jack Knox clinics, started training her, and eventually began entering trials at the novice level. I've always been very competitive—I was a team roper for about 15 years, I ran track and played basketball in high school—so I have always had a competitive nature, and I've always liked dogs and doing stuff outdoors around livestock, and to me it was just the perfect combination of all of my interests with animals, and being competitive, and being an outdoors person. I was lucky—Holly was just a wonderful dog. She had the ability to take a lot of training pressure. And there were a lot of things that I did that were negative things, but because she was strong-natured as far as her temperament, and she wanted to work so badly, she just bounced back from it. It was just wonderful. I really enjoyed running her. A dog like her kind of comes around once in a lifetime, and I'm so glad to have had her and had the experience of working her. She opened up so many doors for me.

Do you take in dogs for training? Or are the dogs you start mostly your own dogs?

Well, over the years I have taken in a lot of dogs. Just through doing demonstrations and stuff, I've trained a lot of farm dogs for people around here. Just put a month or two on them. Basic stops— they don't have to have a big outrun—but if you can get a stop and maybe a little bit of flanking and pace, that type of stuff. I've done quite a bit of that. I have probably only had four or five dogs that I've trained and run for other people. But as a general rule, I've found that I would rather just have my own dogs and train them.

How many dogs do you think that you start a year, on average?

I probably start maybe five or six, depending on the year.

Most of the time I will never breed a litter of puppies that I don't keep two from.

When you choose a puppy, what do you look for? What do you consider the ideal pup?

For me, I like an alert puppy. I like a puppy that comes out looking and trying to see what's going on when it hears a lawnmower going by, or the one that jumps on the fence like, "Hey, what is that all about?" That is what I'm looking for. That's probably also going to be the puppy that eats its fill and pushes the others off to the side. I like a more aggressive dog, one that is a little bit more outgoing. I like to take the puppies to a new environment and just dump them out and see how they all interact. I'll take them to a lot of situations and see which puppy seems to have the most even temperament. It doesn't have to be an aggressive puppy that bites all the others, or anything like that. But I just want a confident, outgoing puppy.

So you tend to go for the alpha pup?

Yes. Holly was that way. There were a couple of puppies that were bigger than Holly in her litter, but she was the one that ate first. She was the first one out of the dog house when I would go to look at them. She was just a little bit more daring, a little bit more courageous, and curious about situations. I am not saying that it is a characteristic that all good dogs have, but it is something that I like to look for. Unfortunately (and I feel fairly confident that out of the litters over the years I've picked some really, really nice puppies), the thing that I've been never able to pick is the amount of eye. That is something that is just a gamble. The eye certainly plays a factor, and some of the puppies that start working really, really young are your strong-eyed dogs. I like a medium amount of eye. I don't like your super stronger-eyed dogs. It seems like they get more and more eye as they get older, and they are harder to move around.

How are your pups raised? Are they house dogs or are they kennel dogs?

As a general rule, my dogs are outside dogs. Now I'll bring puppies in when they're young, and they'll stay in a crate at night. But while I'm watching television, I'll have the puppy out just kind of bouncing around the house, playing and chewing and just kind of doing normal puppy stuff. I think it's important to have a bond with the puppies. I know I kept Holly in the house as a puppy, and she slept in the same room with me. The more interaction you can have with the dogs, the better off you'll be. In a perfect world, I would probably have a puppy in a crate right there in the house with me all of the time. I think you are going to get a stronger bond than if it stays in the kennel with the other dogs.

But you think at some point they should move out to the kennel?

Well, during the day if I don't take the puppy to work, then the puppy will go out into the kennel with the other dogs. It's learning and it is getting well-rounded—it's getting a bit of affection from me and it is also interacting with the other dogs. It's learning to stay outside, and what it's like to be out in the kennel, and, hopefully, as it matures it's learning to stay in a crate and behave without whining and howling and barking. So it learns a little patience.

What do you consider the ideal age for starting your pup on sheep?

I really don't start formal training on one until it is probably ten or twelve months old. Even then, there are exceptions to the rule. Britton, the dog that I'm running right now, was about a year and a half before he was really even ready to take much training pressure. On the other hand, I've had other dogs that at eight months really needed someone to start getting a handle on them. So, it's going to depend on the type of dog that you run and the type of dog that is in your kennel. For my kennel and my dogs, usually by the time they are eight or ten months old, I can get them out and I'm ready to start letting them go around and balance sheep on a regular basis. By that time they have a little bit of a down on them that might not be a hundred percent but is enough to kind of stop them, like a clutch in a car.

Do you let your little puppies just follow you around when you are doing chores and such?

Yes, I do. I let them follow me around until they get keen and want to work. Then at that time, I usually will put them up because most of the time with a four- or five-month-old pup I don't have a lie down or a recall good enough to call it back off a flock of sheep that are running out through the fields. That is one of the reasons I go ahead and expose my puppies to stock. If that puppy is keen at four or five months, by the time I come in and I do all of my chores and I work my older dogs, there really isn't a lot of time for one-on-one time for me and that puppy. But if it's keen and it wants to work, I'll just get it out and let the puppy go around stock. I have several different paddocks and fields that are very much a controlled environment where the sheep can't outrun the puppy and get away from it. The puppy can work, get out of its dog crate and get a little exercise. I also don't have any sheep that are aggressive toward the puppy. And as long as it has an interest and it wants to circle around and do its thing, I'll let it. But at that point, I try not to put any pressure on them.

When do you like them to show an interest in sheep? Do you care? Is there an age where you'd start to worry if you hadn't seen any interest yet?

For me personally, by the time it is ten or twelve months old. I have never had a dog that turned out to be the type I like to run that didn't have an interest in sheep by the time it was that age. But that's me personally. I've had several dogs that were twelve or fourteen months old before they showed an interest in working sheep, and they've made good dogs for other people. And you also have to keep in mind that different bloodlines mature at different levels. It just happens that Holly's bloodline and this Ken Arrendale's Mac line that I have a lot of puppies from now have all started working at an earlier age. But I also think that being able to recognize when a pup can really take the pressures of training is the key to unlocking the door to being able to take puppies to stock at an early age. As long as you can see that, and let me make this important statement, as long as you don't have stock that are going to beat the puppies up, then I don't see how it hurts them. But what so many people do with a pup that turns on by six months and is keen and who wants to work is put pressure on that puppy by the time it is seven or eight months old, by asking it to lie down and to take flanks. Most of the time, this early pressure does as much harm as it does good.

How do you recognize the point where the puppy starts to be ready to take training pressure?

I feel like the puppy is constantly communicating its maturity level to me by the way it's working. There are certain things that I'm really a disciplinarian about when it comes to puppies and dogs in general. I like for them to mind, and I'll be quick to discipline them for some stuff like jumping on me. However, as they start out working, I'll let them push on me. I'll let them get keener and keener, and tougher. Eventually, this will get to the point where the pup is not only just keen and wanting to work, but it's getting more and more into it, as if it's building up a head of steam and getting ready to run downhill. Then I'll ask the puppy to lie down. If it jumps right back up and keeps coming on, then it's handling the pressure. Or maybe I'll ask it to lie down while I'm taking it around the farm next to my four wheeler, and if it comes up fresh and ready and eager to learn then it is ready for that pressure. If every time it gets up slower and slower and acts offended, then that puppy is telling you it is not ready for real training.

Do you ever use any stock other than sheep, like ducks or goats, to start your pups?

I have never used ducks or goats to start a puppy, though I have worked my dogs on goats. Sheep are what I've always had, and sheep are what I have always used to start a pup.

What sort of sheep do you like to use in the beginning? How many do you like to use for starting a pup?

I usually like to have eight or ten nice dog-broke sheep for starting a pup. I'm a little bit partial to wool sheep. It's not that I have anything against hair sheep, but wool sheep are not quite as excitable as hair sheep. I prefer some nice old Dorset ewes that are docile, calm, and quiet, with a good flocking instinct and are just going to walk or trot around. They don't excite a dog as much, they don't play with a dog's eye. Barbados sheep, and some of the other hair breeds that are really fast and flighty, even some of the Cheviots, will almost light up and go on fire when a young puppy comes around. I have the Rambouillet sheep right now that are fairly dog-broke, and unless they have baby lambs I don't have to worry about them turning around and stomping at a dog. If the pup doesn't seem ready to take the pressure of the lie down, I'll add more sheep so the pressure to slow the dog down is coming from the sheep rather than from me.

Do you ever make use of a round pen?

I have a round pen, and I have a smaller lot that I train in. But as a general rule, any pup I work will first turn on to stock while it is out there with me working my older dogs in a big pasture. When I see that puppy first turn on, I will have an older dog out there with it to keep the sheep from totally running away. Again, these are dog-broke sheep that are wanting to stay together. This is where I'll start the puppy basically just kind of circling the stock. Sometimes a really small area, such as a round pen, can actually put more pressure on a dog. If you've ever been around horses, I'll use this example: one of the scariest places that you can be with a horse is not out in an open field but in the horse trailer. When those horses are all jammed up there tight, you can get mashed by a horse up against the trailer. Well, those puppies can sometimes look at a round pen in the same manner. They don't want to go in between the stock and the fence, that's a tight place with a lot of pressure where the sheep might gain an advantage and smash the puppy up against a fence. So as a general rule, I like to start my pups out in a big area. They are pretty much free and they don't have to worry about going in between the stock and the fence or a panel. Now if you have dogs that are bad grippers or you can't catch them, I'd certainly put them into a round pen.

So do you use an older dog to help you with training generally?

Yes, I do. The right type of sheep and an older dog are two important factors for me. Holly did a wonderful job at that. She would lie down there and stay and I would work the puppies. If the sheep got strung out or if the puppy came in and busted them all up, Holly would be right there to put things back in place for me.

How long do you use an older dog?

I usually use an older dog until I feel like I can wear sheep around with the puppy. The puppy needs to have good enough balance and be keen and eager enough that if the sheep get strung out it can tuck in the corners and keep them all together. At that time, I'll just put the older dog up and I'll take the puppy out on its own.

Do you find that it is confusing for the older dog at all?

Yeah, I don't think it is good for them. I mean, I certainly wouldn't do it with the Open dog that I'm going to be competing with at the trial that weekend. You are asking that dog to lie down there and just watch sheep go back and forth. Whether you know it or not, you are changing that dog's eye. That dog is reacting to the things that you do in a different manner, and the next thing you know it'll be cheating on you, getting up on its own, covering on its own, and using its eye in the wrong way. I don't recommend that people use their good Open dog to do that sort of work on a regular basis. It doesn't hurt them every now and then, but an older, retired dog or a farm dog is really the best choice for this sort of work.

What do you like your puppies to know before you introduce them to stock? Do you teach them any commands off sheep?

Before I ever take the puppy to stock, it's going to know its name, it's going to come when it's called, and it's going to know a correction. My puppies will recognize a verbal correction, whether you say, "no" or "ahhh" or "what are you doing?" From the time they're tiny, I start calling them by name, and if they're doing something they shouldn't be doing, I give them a verbal correction, "no" or "ah," whatever you want to use as long as you're consistent and as long as it is going to be something you can do in a hurry. Personally, I don't worry about having a down command on my pups before I take them to stock. Having said this, I also think that it's fine if you want to teach the pup a down command as long as you don't do it with too much pressure—you are interacting, communicating, and building a bond with that puppy. Whether doing obedience, dog tricks or whatever, all of these things are the start of you and puppy becoming a team.

Do you ever use any tools when you train, like a whip, or a pvc pipe, rattle paddle, or anything like that?

Basically, I will either carry a crook or sometimes a longe whip, which is a little more flexible than a white stick. There are several reasons I like the longe whip: you can wiggle it back and forth and make a kind of whooshing noise, you can also smack it on the ground a little more easily if you are trying to keep a dog back, and you can rake it back and forth in front of the sheep.

What do you like to see in a pup's first few sessions? What would tell you that a pup's a good prospect, what might warn you of later problems?

I like to see a puppy that is willing to go around and circle the stock. I don't like to see a pup lie down and just stare, stare, stare. This tells me that there is some eye revealing itself. I don't like to see a puppy run by sheep, bite, and then run away from the stock. I've had puppies that would do that. They never seem really to balance the stock, all they want to do is fly in, take a bite, and run away. I don't like that. I like to see a puppy that will get in behind the stock and constantly keep working the balance. I don't mind if they bite heels or bite them on the nose or bite them on the side—that doesn't really bother me at all. I like to see a puppy that is willing to put pressure on sheep constantly. I like to be able to back eight or ten sheep up along the fence and see what that puppy's reaction is. Does it get back there a distance away and lie down and look at the stock? Does it come in there to ten yards and stand up on its feet, ready to work, and kind of go back and forth like a cutting horse keeping them all up against the fence? Does it walk right in, grab one, and turn around and run away? Or does it just walk right in nose-to-nose with the sheep just three or four inches away? All of those things are telling you something about that pup's level of confidence. Once the sheep are standing quietly up against the fence, some trainers like to see a dog lie down on its own. There is absolutely nothing wrong with that, but what I really like are the pups that are always eager to put a little bit more pressure on the stock. That is what I'm looking for. After the puppy gets comfortable balancing the sheep, one of the first things I'll do is put sheep up against a corner and see how close a puppy will come in. From there, I'll step aside and see if that puppy is willing to come in between the stock and the fence on its own.

Is there a pup that you trained that stands out in your mind as having shown the most early promise, and did that dog end up being as promising as it looked like it would be when it first started out?

Looking back on it, Holly was all of the things that I'm looking for, but I didn't realize it at the time. She seemed to have the things that I mentioned above. I think about times when I'd put Holly into those positions, and she was the one to dive in there and peel them off the fence, constantly wanting to put pressure on the stock. McCloud was a lot more timid around stock until he was about ten months old, but from then on he was diving in there, pulling them out of the corner, just crawling and digging under the sheep and the fence. Holly and McCloud in particular, from the time they were ten to twelve months old, couldn't get close enough to the sheep—they were always wanting to put pressure on them. A lot of people wouldn't like that, a lot of people like to see them get back and find a natural balance and find that natural pace and just kind of keep that same distance. There again, there is nothing at all wrong with that, people have different preferences and different styles and ways of running dogs.

So the type that you prefer might not necessarily come along easily at the beginning, they might be tougher as puppies, but you like what you get in the end better?

Yes, and I'll tell you why. I keep referring back to Holly because she was the dog that I trained when I had the least amount of knowledge, but I think about the Nursery dogs that she ran against as a two and three year old, and there weren't but three or four that were still running and winning trials at eleven the way Holly was. When Holly was ten and eleven she won more trials those couple of years than she ever did as a younger dog. She really didn't settle down and start winning Open trials consistently until she was five. That's a long time to wait. There are puppies that get to five and are easy to handle and nice, good Open dogs, but then by seven or eight they just seem to disappear. So the type of dog I'm looking for is not going to be as good a young dog—I've never had really competitive Nursery dogs—but they'll be good, competitive older dogs. To me, when people are retiring their dogs at eight or nine, I think of Holly giving me three more great years. This kind of bonus is what you get, running the type of dogs that I run. I think this says a lot about the dog's character, desire to work, and mental toughness. And that's why I like the stronger-natured dogs: I think in the end they're going to last longer.

Why don't you talk a little bit about your progression of training phases and how you train? What skills do you start with, when do you like to move on to the new skill? How does it work?

I start with the puppies by letting them learn to bring sheep to me. When they are comfortable with that, then I'll start asking them to lie down. When they are comfortable doing that, I'll lie them down and then I'll let the sheep drift off away from us a little bit, then start shushing them around on a small outrun, maybe ten yards. I stand in between the puppy and the sheep and shush it, until the pup gets comfortable with that little bit of pressure with me standing between it and the stock. As it start to that, I'll watch it and see if it gets up and streaks toward the sheep trying to get to them by running through my legs in a mad dash, or does it have that natural cast around the stock. If it has the natural cast, it is telling me, "There's no need to push me off right now. I'm young, and I've got a natural cast about me. So, there's no need to put a lot of unnecessary pressure on me." If the pup tells me that it can take the pressure, then I'll carry on. If not, then I'll just simply go back and continue wearing a little bit more. If the puppy is not ready to take the training pressure, I'm not going to put it in a situation where it constantly fails. I just simply let it continue doing what it is willing to give me, eventually reintroducing small amounts of pressure to see how the dog reacts. During this time I am asking myself the question, do I like this dog? Is it progressing at a level that is acceptable? Or would my time be better spent on another dog? When the pup is doing a little outrun, I'll let it wear sheep, and then send it on another little outrun in the other direction. When it learns to bring sheep to me from fifty yards away, or seventy-five yards away, or maybe even a hundred yards away, only then will I start to teach its sides, when I'm confident that the dog knows that bringing me sheep is what it's been bred to do.

How do you go about lengthening and shaping the outrun?

Going back to that correction that I taught that puppy before I ever took it to stock, I'll lie the dog down and give it that correction. I'll use whatever correction the dog is familiar with when it's not doing right. I'll lie the dog down, I'll get between the dog and the stock, and I'll growl at it or say, "What are you doing?" or I'll use that longe whip and I'll just kind of point it at the dog—I'm using both verbal language and body language to communicate to the dog that it's wrong. The dog will have the same reaction to me that it would to an alpha dog chasing it off a kill: it'll turn its head away and submit to my pressure. If it comes in tight again, I'm going to stop it, I'm going to get between it and the stock and I'm going to growl like I'm the alpha and it's way down there in the pecking order. Because it knows its correction, it is going to give ground and cast out again.

When do you start insisting on absolute obedience, and how do you balance absolute obedience with developing the pup's initiative and confidence?

Really, that obedience starts at a very, very young age. If I'm sitting there on the floor watching television and the puppy is chewing on my sock and I say, "no" or "what are you doing, puppy?" and if it looks up at me and goes right back to chewing up my sock, I might give that puppy a little flick on the nose. That puppy says, "Man, when he says that and I didn't stop doing what I was doing, he gives me a little thump." So, I've really started this obedience from the time they are puppies in the form of a little discipline. And as the puppy gets older, of course, it is able take more pressure, but at the same time the pressure gets harder the more time you have to ask it. To get back to your question, if a dog is keen and it wants to work and it wants to get to the stock, the only way it's going to get to that stock is by taking the pressure and doing it the right way. That's the way I punish the dog. I'm taking the stock away from it by stepping between the dog and its sheep. I'm taking away the fun. The only way that it gets the fun back, is to give when I put pressure on it. It doesn't take them long to learn, even the strong dogs, that once you say lie down and you start growling, there is no way that dog is going to get to the stock until it submits and obeys my command. And that's the way you see dogs that are flexible and dogs that will bend and really give on their flanks and widen out on their outrun. That's the way you get dogs to stop that are out 200 yards away and they're lost but can take nice, big redirects on their outruns. They've been taught to bend, just like a horse would arch its neck and give its head to the bit. It's been taught to take pressure and give to the pressure. Same thing with the dogs on these outruns. When they're old enough and keen enough, they're not going to get there until they do as I ask. How much I demand will depend on the strength of the dog, the age of the dog, and a lot of times the blood lines, too. Some dogs will develop a natural cast about them as they get older. I'm not going to push that dog out as much as a young dog as I would a really strong dog with tight flanks. Dogs that are not good flankers or outrunners—I'm going to push those out harder at an early age.

How do you introduce the drive?

I usually let the dog wear the sheep right up to me, and as the sheep go around me I'll call the dog to me, bend down, and just pet it. I never start driving until the dog is good at fetching and bringing sheep to me and will come off sheep when called. At that point, I simply start walking with the dog behind the stock. I let that dog do anything it wants to do as long as it doesn't go past 3:00 or 9:00 with me standing at about 6:00. So now, it still has 180 degrees to do anything it wants: bite, run, walk, trot, whatever. When it gets to 3:00 or 9:00, I will say, "Ah ah," or "no," anything to let it know where that boundary is. I'll use the dog's name for inside flanks or to get it to come back to me. So, if the dog is going out there to 3:00, I'll call it back to me, "that'll do, here," then "walk up." Then it learns to walk and wear sheep just like it did to bring them to you, only now they are wearing sheep away from you with that same 180 degree boundary. It can do anything it wants, as long as it doesn't go past 3:00 or 9:00. If it starts to get close there, I'll give it a little correction, and it learns that as long as it stays within that boundary there is not a lot of discipline. They don't have to stand or walk or lie down or march like a soldier. Even though I run my dogs with a lot of discipline on them, I don't really start that way with the training, that comes later. I don't use a line. I feel like if I have to use a line on the dog, to keep it back there or to *make it* stay back there, I don't have the right kind of bond with that dog or I'm putting that dog in over its head.

How about shedding? How early do you introduce shedding? How do you go about that?

I will introduce shedding usually after I have the dog outrunning, familiar with its flanks, and driving some. Most all of my Nursery dogs are familiar with shedding, even though they might not be experts at it. I don't think there is anything wrong with introducing the shed to a dog that maybe hasn't even learned to drive. If I've got 150 sheep out there and I see an opportunity where some go one way and some go another, I'll just drop down on my knees and call the dog straight to me and pet it. It doesn't realize it, but that's one of the first steps to the shed. So I'll always take advantage of that opportunity when it comes about, but I think I would *never* do anything with a shed until I had a good recall on a dog to where it would come to me readily.

How about whistles? When do you introduce the dog to whistles? Do you use different sets for different sorts of dogs?

I do; I like to pick a set of whistles that suits the dog. If I've got a fast, hyper, quick-natured dog, I like to use the slower, more drawn-out whistles. If it is a little more of a sluggish slow-flanker, or a dog with a lot of eye, then I'll use quick, exciting, fast whistles for the dog. Out of habit I start whistling quite early to my dogs. I do the whistle and verbal almost one with another from the time they are very young.

At what point do you start entering your young dogs in trials, and what do you want to get out of those early trials for training experiences?

I don't ever enter a dog in a trial until I feel that I can be competitive with that dog. If you adopt this mentality, then you will not put the dog in over its head. The most important thing at those early trials is that the dog learns that it has to behave away from home just like it does at home.

Is that for the good of the dog or because of what you prefer to show up with?

It is for the good of the dog; it really has nothing to do with me. I've learned that this is a pretty humbling sport, and I'm not really prideful when it comes to the dogs. They can really make a fool out of you in a hurry. I feel like you're setting precedents for the future and the dog is learning that he can get away with away from home. I've bought dogs that people have run too early, and I have seen people expose dogs to trials too early. It doesn't take long for these dogs to figure out that at home you have to mind and away from home you don't. If you can't make that dog walk with you to the post, without having it on a leash, how are you going to control that dog even on a pro-novice or novice outrun at 75 yards? I don't believe in taking dogs out early, just to get experience or just to get their feet wet and stuff. I feel like they need to have a good solid foundation and they need to be trained and then you can introduce something the dogs to trialing.

What is the most important tip that you would like to pass on to others who are interested in training a puppy, maybe even their first puppy?

When picking a puppy, I would try to follow the training routine and the bloodlines and the training tips of a handler with a similar temperament to yours who handles a dog the way that you would like to handle, and with somebody that runs the type of dog that you think you would be interested in running. I think a lot of people start off with dogs that are mismatched for them, and it just makes for a bad team. It sets a mood where the people won't enjoy the dog like they should. I've wasted a lot of time trying puppies from people who work their dogs completely differently from me. If you are a quiet, calm-natured person that only gets to work sheep on the weekends, try to get a dog from someone who isn't a hill shepherd or a farmer for a living. You can't take a soft-natured dog to somebody who is a really heavy-handed trainer and expect to have much success. Just like you can't take a really strong, hard dog to somebody who is used to working very soft, quiet-tempered dogs. Picking the right dog and the right trainer and method is beneficial to most novices. I know it would have benefited me.

Julie Hill

HERIOT, SCOTLAND

Julie Hill is an internationally-respected judge and handler, as well as the author of the highly acclaimed training book The Natural Way. *A veteran competitor of many sheepdog trials, Julie won the 1991 Scottish National Championship with her bitch Gwen and the 1996 International Supreme Championship with her dog Moss.*

"Every time a dog is working on sheep, it is actually talking to us. It is telling us what is happening and what you need to help it with."

*How long have you been involved in sheepdog training and
trialing? How did it happen for you?*

I suppose it would be over twenty years. I think it was in 1984
or '82 that I had my first pup. I worked with horses before
that, and there was an accidental birth on the farm. I always
loved dogs, so it seemed natural when I had this pup and she
was desperate to work anything—geese, horses, or sheep.

*So it was a pup born to a bitch owned by someone else on
the farm?*

Yes, it was an accidental birth when two farm dogs got together. This was my ideal opportunity to get my first-ever
dog. I always loved dogs as a kid but was never allowed to
have one.

And you had sheep?

Well, there were sheep on the farm. So eventually I ended up
with the sheep becoming my work. This dog and I worked
together trying to learn the ropes until we went for professional help.

And how did that work, training your dog yourself?

She was a plain-eyed dog, a real good farm dog. She was quite
clever. She did a lot of things that were clever that I wouldn't
have known were clever at the time, but she just helped. We
had originally worked on river banks; I didn't need a dog to
gather, just drive, and so when I found myself with sheep in a
field, I had no outrun on my dog. Fortunately, I heard of help
through the Agricultural Training Board for sheepdog training and decided to give it a go to see if my dog and I could be
helped.

Do you take in dogs for training, or are you starting dogs as prospective sheepdogs for your own work and trial needs?

We have about 600 acres and 500 sheep. I take in dogs to train, and do clinics, and take people in for teaching, and, of course, train a few of my own.

How many dogs do you start a year on average?

Oh, it's hard to say. If you were speaking about me taking in other people's pups to start, maybe about ten, maybe more. It varies, you know, because I'm working in clinics all of the time, helping start dogs all of the time. For my own, I only like to keep two or three and work through them and decide what I'm going to keep from that.

What do you look for in a puppy? What do you consider the ideal pup?

Well for me, I just like something with a bit of a character. Looking real sharp. Mischievous really, but in a nice way. I just like them really keen, mischievous, and obviously good looks helps, but it doesn't matter much to me, I just like something with a bit of character.

What do you consider "good looks"? What physical type of border collie do you like?

I quite like a short-coated and prick-eared dog. I mean, anything is good if it has got a brain. I do like an athletic kind of dog. I don't like too big a dog. I want something that is as tight-skinned as possible, prick-eared, and just really athletic—whippety-looking, really. But they are not all that way, and the dogs obviously are a bit bigger than that. But I'm more for a short than a long coat.

How do you raise your pups? Are they house dogs or kennel dogs?

They're brought up in the kennel. I usually like to bring them up on their own to bond with me. But because of my situation now I often bring two pups up together so they've got company. As they get a bit older, I split them up and start getting a bit more personal with them. But when they are very small I like them to have that bit of company in the kennel, and they keep each other warm. They come out with the rest of the dogs, and they run together as a pack. Not all the time, but they go out for walks together. They join in the pack right at the beginning. I'm often taking out a large number of dogs, and I like every dog to accept each other, with me as the boss.

Do you let your pups follow you around as you are doing chores to introduce them to stock? Or do you like to keep them separate from stock until you are ready to begin formal training?

It depends what I'm doing, but . . . no. If it was a pup on its own, I'm more likely to let it come with me when I'm doing, not really jobs with stock, little things like tidying up a shed or something. It is different. It has changed now from what I did when I was actually working as a shepherd on the hill and I only had my own dogs, I had a few with me, and the dogs were with me every minute of the day that I was out. That was just a different way of bringing them up. Now I've moved and I have a lot more things that need to be done a lot faster, so I don't have as much time. So it depends on your situation, and my situation just now has changed slightly. I try to handle the dogs as much as possible, but sometimes they are really not getting a lot to do until they've grown up a bit.

When do you like to see pups start to show an interest in sheep? Does it matter to you?

I certainly like to see them show an interest, but I don't like to put them on stock too young. You know, six to seven months is really early enough for me. Between seven, eight to twelve months is the goal for starting to be really serious about doing something with them. Before that I like to show them, just to be sure they are going to be interested. I try to teach them basic commands off sheep before I go to sheep.

So what about that, what kind of commands do you like to teach them before they go to sheep?

Just coming back, lying down—just manners really to get their respect. You need to start building that respect right as puppies. You know, to come into the kennels when they are called, to come with you when you are on a walk. And they will go through that time when they'll try you out, and think, "All right, I'm going to not behave today. I'm going to go off looking for sheep. I'm going to do something." And you just have to work through that, get them on a long line, and teach them that no, they are not going to have this, they are going to have to come with you. But really seriously starting to take them out every day or every other day will be at about eight months—if they are interested enough at that time. I like to know that they are going to work. I don't keep anything much over twelve months if it's not showing any interest.

Is there an age that you think a dog is too old to get started? If one of your clients came to you with an older dog, is there an age that you'd think it wasn't even worth trying to get it started?

No, not really. It depends on how natural the dog is, and the instinct that is in it and how clever it is. The only thing I would say is that you've got that window of opportunity where the dogs learn a lot more easily between the age of a year and three years. It doesn't mean that they can't learn later, but it is like ourselves, when you're younger you can absorb more quickly and you can learn more easily; as you start to get older it takes more time to learn the same thing, and that's how it is with dogs, too. And because you've got a shorter lifespan in a dog, you've only got until they're nine to ten years, so you've really got to put as much time in that year to three years so that you've got the experience put in by the time they get to be three and four year olds. The older a dog is who has formed bad habits, the harder those problems are to cure.

Why don't you describe your first couple of sessions with a pup. Do you like a very controlled environment? Do you use a round pen? What are you doing in the first couple of sessions?

I like to keep close to the sheep and to encourage the dog to balance sheep to me. I might use a round pen, but I tend to prefer an older dog to hold sheep to me in a small field and try to keep it quite controlled. I like to keep on the sheep and try to encourage the dog to balance sheep to me.

How many sheep do you like to use?

I'll probably only use five or six at that real small age, because if you get too many they start splitting and it encourages the pup just to chase. So, not too many sheep.

Do you ever use stock other than sheep, like goats or ducks?

No. I've used ducks before. It was okay, it worked quite well, the only thing is—it might have been because of the type of dog I had—the dog was actually flanking quite tight. It took me awhile to push her off of sheep after working her on ducks, but that was probably just the fact that she was going to be inclined that way anyway.

Do you use any training aids or other equipment?

I like a pvc plastic pipe as my main one; I will take a whip out. But mainly I'm using it just as an extension of my arm, just to be able to put the pressure at the point at the right time. It gives you that bit of extra length. And the plastic pipe I use to make that extra bit of noise on your wellie. It's the same thing, to get the timing of the pressure right. To encourage the dogs to give to pressure, basically.

What do you like to see in a pup's first few sessions? What would excite you and make you think the pup was going to be a good prospect? What might concern you?

I like to see something that is not too wide off sheep, that is getting on with it, with really good balance. I want them to be balancing sheep to me, *really* enthusiastic, and coming forward. I like to see nice turns on the dog, and a good tail that is well tucked in. Pups can throw their tail up to start with, but after awhile I like to see it where it should be. In general, I like to see balance, a good tail, and a dog showing good natural ability.

What would raise red flags if you were seeing it in the first couple of sessions?

Something that would lie down and just stare at the sheep, something that you would struggle to move. The gripping, that's a questionable one. It doesn't really matter if it's a puppy grip. It is something that I would keep an eye on, but it's not something that would alarm me. Mainly that stickiness, not wanting to come forward, not wanting to come near sheep. Fleeing too far off its sheep would be another alarm; I would not want to see that at that age.

Do you find that the dogs that you start that train up really easily end up being the better dogs in the end, or do you think that you can't really generalize?

I've had both. I've had ones that have trained up easy and become good, and I've had ones that have been a handful and become good. It depends what ability they have that you can bring out. I mean, I quite like a strong dog, something that is going to push on, a pushy kind of dog. I like a tryer and something that will give you its heart in its work. I like a dog with stamina that is going to be able to run for long periods of time. But I think that even if a dog can be pushy, it can still be easy to train. So it depends how you define easy to train. I don't personally like too much having to encourage a dog every step of the way because when it comes to working you are wanting them to think for themselves and be pushing on and doing a lot of natural stuff. So that can be a mixed answer depending on how you read the question, I think. What I'm looking for is a dog with stamina, natural ability, trainability, and good temperament.

Now think about the best dog that you've ever trained. Was that dog easy to train or was that dog more difficult to train? And who was that dog?

Well, I can tell you a few of the best ones and tell you how they were, which might give you an idea. One of my first ones was Gwen. I liked her; as a pup she was very mischievous and full of fun, always smiling at you to get her own way. But she was so willing. You could train her every minute of the day, and she never soured. She just loved it. She loved any chance she could get to work. She was quite strong in the fact that she didn't like to stop too much, she liked to come on, but she was easy and she was natural.

So she trained up really easily?

She trained up really easily. She had the right kind of room. The only thing she had was that she was strong, and she took a bit of stopping. So you had to get her respect quite a bit. But she had the right feel. She was the only dog that I've had that, right from the beginning, would always be a hundred percent correct at the top of the field whatever type of sheep she had—she could lift heavy, she could lift light, and she just had the real feel for sheep. I suppose she would be my best one for that. But she had her faults, too. Now, Moss, he was a tremendous athlete. He had great stamina. But he was more sensitive, so he was harder to train. He taught me that I had to give and take more. I could have been too hard with pressure at certain times with Gwen, but she would forgive me, she never worried. Her nature was that good that it never bothered her. Moss would let you know if you'd overstepped the mark.

So how easy was Moss to train?

He was a devil and got up to a lot of things that he probably shouldn't have, but without this spirit he would have been dull. He would push sheep too hard often, and if he saw a chance he would chase one sheep down to the other end of the field. And then he wouldn't allow you to be too hard in terms of correction. So you really had to learn how to give this pressure and release at just the right time. But experience taught him. He was always a classy, smart-looking dog, right at the beginning. He had a lot of qualities that I probably took for granted at that time.

Now if you were plugging away with a dog that just wasn't making satisfactory progress, is there a point at which you would say that this dog isn't worth bothering with?

Yes, the biggest thing that helped me with training dogs is to actually look at what they are able to do. Not every dog can make a trial dog. Not every dog can make a talented work dog. All the dogs have got their particular amount of gift, and you have to decide at some point, well this one can't stand the pressure of training for trials, or that one hasn't got enough push to go to someone with a heap of sheep, or this one isn't clever enough to work on the hill. You've got to decide what that dog is very good at and what it is not very good at. I usually then sell them to places where I know they are going to be satisfied, where I know they are going to fit in. I think that helped me, because when I first started I thought every one could train to a trial dog standard, and they can't—not everyone has the ability for that. So actually it takes the pressure off you as a handler if you accept that every dog has its own talents. I take them as far as I can take them. But experience will tell you how far you can take a dog. If you really want a dog that can be a hell of a workdog and can work to international trial standards, that will take a lot of training, and some dogs just don't have the temperament to take it.

Why don't you describe your basic phases of training that you use when you are starting a pup?

Well, first of all, I just want them to be able to wear and hold sheep. Balance a hundred percent, so that I can walk off and let them balance sheep to me. Then I'm gradually flanking them behind me at this stage, just walking off and getting them to take the flank naturally away from me and then behind me. It is basically the same thing, but you're just moving across the line to get them to flank behind you, rather than away from you. But I set off walking a lot at that early stage, doing small turns, getting them to balance. And once that balancing work is done, I'll be starting to stop them a bit. Making them listen to commands, flanking them to commands.

How do you go about lengthening and shaping the outrun?

Well, that's a gradual process. Basically, coming from when you taught them balance, you'd gradually lengthen it to where you stood in the middle between the dog and its sheep, and just gradually develop it. And the dog will near enough show you how natural it is on the outrun. I analyze my dog right from the beginning on how it is balancing and how it is moving its sheep, and then I'll actually decide how I'm going to train it based on what I'm seeing, depending on the strengths and weaknesses that I see. So I might have to work more on the balance, or the dog might be too wide off and I need to work on actually keeping contact. A lot of the training stages are based on what I'm analyzing as I'm going along. But obviously, first of all, you start on balance, then you teach a small outrun. Then I'll teach a natural fetch and drive, which actually encourages them to drive in their own personal manner. Once I've got the dog flanking behind me, I'll teach them to drive in a square. So you don't have to have the outrun really big, but you have to have things all very correct before you go on to the driving. I'll teach the drive in a square first before I'll actually do driving in front of me.

When do you introduce the stop and the steady?

The stop and the steady come very quickly once you have respect. I'm looking at setting a foundation that will be with the dog for the rest of his life. So everything you are doing at this early stage is building up for the final picture. Once the dog understands pressure and release, stopping and steadying becomes easy for the dog to understand. I am asking the dog to steady right at the beginning, and once I know that the dog has respect for the sheep and for me as a handler, I ask for the stop. This foundation is the most important stage of training a dog. Basically, I'm teaching them to give to pressure and release, and also to understand the communication between you and the dog. In fact, teaching the dog to communicate with me is probably the most important stage of training. I'm teaching it how to give to pressure and how, when I release, to feel that it can come forward. It is the same with the "ask," "tell," and "insist" commands. You have to know how you are going to ask the dog, tell the dog, and insist, actually to communicate what is right and wrong with that dog. So you have all of this in place before you do much training. They've actually got to have a feel of it. So everything that you are doing at this basic stage is kind of building up for the bigger picture.

When, if ever, do you start insisting on absolute obedience in your commands?

I do it in a natural way in the sense that I ask, tell, and insist. I teach a dog. You've got actually to give the dog time to learn something. You've got to teach it, and you have to be consistent in the way you are teaching it. So, say I'm teaching a flank. I'm shushing it to start with and pushing it away from me using that pressure to encourage it to run away to the one side. Then I'll stop it and encourage it to go the other way. Well, I'll do that for quite awhile. I'll teach it; I'll spend awhile teaching it. Then I'll actually wean off the body language a bit and start to test that it is listening to my voice. And that is why I always use my voice in the ask, tell, and insist mode, and you just go up and down the octaves to tell them right from wrong. But what I'll do is that once I know that they know what I mean, then I'll start to put a little bit more pressure on that they have to start to listen. But that doesn't mean that I'm going to jump to an "insist" mode, I'm just trying to get them to understand how to listen. Once they listen and if I think they are defying me, then I insist. But if they are not defying me, if they are trying, then I'm still working away asking and telling them. But when I know they know better and they defy me, then I'll go on to the "insist."

Do you find it hard to balance the need for obedience with the desire to build a pup's initiative and confidence?

I think that that's the hardest lesson for a beginner to learn. How to feel what a dog should do naturally without over controlling it, but yet have enough control through respect. Respect is the most important thing a person can learn, because it is not about obedience. You have to teach a dog respect through pressure release. Once you have, it knows how to give and release to you, but then you have to be consistent to get what you want, and you have to *know* what you want to get it. But if you get your respect, you have a better feel between you and your dog. It is not you controlling, it is not him taking over. It is the two of you working as a team. If you get that balance right at the beginning, you can actually see it developing right at that early stage, that communication. That is why I spend more time at that basic stage. And with a beginner, too, or most people that come to me for lessons, I go back to that basic stage so they can learn how it feels when the dog gives its respect to you. The dog knows it is allowed to think for itself, but if you give it a command it will do as you say. That is the way I work, and depending on the dog I will decide how much I'll let it think and how much I'll make it do what I want.

How do you handle faults that come up in young dogs, such as a dog that grips or chases?

Pressure and release again is the only way to correct any fault. How bad the grip is will determine how much pressure I'll have to put on the dog to correct it. Basically, I'm wanting that dog to give to my pressure, body language or voice. You wean onto voice eventually. So if you are telling a dog to get out, you have to teach it how to give to that pressure on the word "out." So say they are coming in for a grip, at that point before the grip you need to push them out at the shoulder and teach the dog to get out. Now the amount of pressure you have to apply will depend on the nature of the dog. A lot of dogs are taught to come to pressure and not give to pressure. Say I was teaching my dog to give to pressure and I wanted it to go away and it gave to me. So I then released it and let it come onto its sheep. Now suddenly I pushed it again and it went too far and I wanted it to stop. Now I've seen people run at the dog to get it to stop. Well, if that dog learned its lesson correctly, going toward it should make it leave, not stop. And some people go towards it and say, "Now you better stop." Well, all that's doing is confusing it because one minute you've taught it to leave on pressure and now you are telling it to stop on pressure. So I never fall out with the stop. I cut them off, I don't allow them to get sheep, but I actually block them from getting the sheep until they stop. So that is the pressure, basically, you aren't letting, but I don't go towards them to get them to stop. So, sometimes that battle of communication is the problem. Basically you have to break that down and re-teach them the pressure and release technique to get them to stop gripping, if that is the problem. But not every dog you can stop from gripping, it depends why it is gripping; it might be coarse, or weak, or confused and just getting mixed up.

How do you go about teaching the drive?

Mainly, I teach them how to push sheep first on this natural fetch and drive. I'll let sheep go in front of me and I'll let the dogs flank to keep sheep turned in at the corners. I'll use a bigger bunch of sheep, and I'll take sheep for quite some way and try to get the dogs to push them past me, learn them how to actually push sheep and take sheep. A lot of times dogs don't know how to take sheep. They can fetch sheep but they can't take sheep and push them. So, once they learn that then I start to drive in a square.

What do you want them to know before you start teaching the drive?

How to push sheep, basically, in the direction you want to go. How to make sheep go from a walk to a trot. They have to know the concept of the drive, this basic concept of how to take sheep this way when you are walking that way. So I am with the dog, but the sheep are often in front of me and the dog is flanking, turning in the sides, and taking sheep in the direction that I'm walking. And once they know that idea, it is much easier for them to drive in a square and the more precision driving comes in. But I do then add with the steady a stand command rather than a lie down. I try to keep the flow going so they can get a feel of it.

How early do you introduce shedding?

Quite early. I've usually got them doing everything at close level, basically, and if they are doing everything well—small outruns and doing quite a bit of driving—then I'll go into shedding quite early. It depends again on the dog. If the dogs are not covering sheep properly, then I wouldn't be shedding because I don't want to encourage them not to cover the sheep. It depends on the amount of eye they've got and their faults, what I'm trying to put right. If shedding at a young age would make it worse, then I wouldn't do it. But otherwise I would do it quite early on.

How about whistles? Do you introduce them early? Do you use the same set of whistles for all of your dogs, or do you sometimes use different whistles depending on certain qualities of the dog?

I'll use different sets of whistles mainly because I'll try to work a brace dog. Sometimes I'll have three sets of whistles. At work I'll take three or four dogs often, so it is handy if you've got them on different sets of whistles. But I do try to pick what whistles I think would suit that dog if possible, sometimes you just need to just pick a set that allows you to work it with another dog. But if you've got a real fast dog, I don't want to be giving him sharp, quick whistles, I'll want a set of whistles to try to steady him down. And the same goes with a slow dog, I'll want to give him snappier whistles to sharpen him up.

So how early do you start whistles in your program?

I would like to start them very early. I would like to put them on whistles right at the beginning of putting them on flank commands. But because I cannot whistle through my teeth or by using my fingers, I have to rely on a plastic whistle. Since taking the whistle in and out of my mouth irritates me, I personally train on voice first before putting them on whistles. But you can do it as early as you like, and I would like to be starting them on whistles a lot sooner than I personally do.

At what point do you like to start entering your young dog in trials? What do you like to get out of these early trials?

I quite like the Nursery trials, although it is hard when you are in competition not to put pressure on a dog. We're talking about, in our country, dogs who are two and a half go into the Nurseries. If the dog is ready, it'll go in. If it is not ready, then I won't bother, I'll leave it for a year. It doesn't bother me if it is not going to be ready. It is good to get young dogs out to this kind of level to work out all of the daft stuff that you are going to get, like taking sheep off other people. And since we have to shed in our Nurseries, you need to get them to that point if you want to compete.

Is that just true in Scotland?

Yes, mainly Scotland. I think there is shedding in some parts of England, too, but there are a lot of trials in England that don't even shed in the Open. It just all depends on what area you are in, but in Scotland you definitely shed in the Nurseries. Which is good. They don't make it any more difficult than necessary, usually it is four sheep and you are just splitting them—you don't have to go to the last single. You are making it quite simple. But I quite like the Nurseries if the dog is able, although I certainly don't take the dog if it isn't ready.

If you had to pass on one tip to people training dogs, maybe even someone training a first dog, what would that tip be? What is the most important thing that you would like to tell trainers of border collies?

Learning how to get communication and respect from the dog. Every time a dog is working on sheep, it is actually talking to us. It is telling us what is happening and what you need to help it with. I think just getting that basic understanding and communication with your dog would be the biggest breakthrough for any beginner. To get that respect, get that feel, and feel like you've bonded right from the beginning, and feel good about the start. If you are not feeling good at the start, you are not going to feel good further on, because if you haven't got that respect, you haven't got anything. I would say spend a lot of time working out how to communicate and reading your dog.

Carla King

DAVIDSONVILLE, MARYLAND

Carla King has been involved in sheepdogs for the past twenty years. She began as a novice with her self-trained bitch Pride, who proved enormously talented; Carla and Pride enjoyed much success in trials throughout the Southeast. Carla is currently trialing sparingly but successfully, as well as giving lessons to novice trainers, taking young dogs in for training, and running her own working farm.

"You need a relationship with your dog for training: it helps to love your dog, but you also need to teach your dog to respect you."

How many dogs do you start a year?

I may start one for myself, and I usually start an average of about six for other people.

What do you look for when you choose a puppy?

That's hard to say—I kind of like to let the puppy choose me. Obviously, before they're born I'm going to have to like the mother and father. After that, any pup that catches my eye is what I'll take. I usually tend to pick females for some reason; I'm not sure why, but that's what I seem to prefer.

Do you have any physical characteristics that you prefer in your pups?

I don't worry much about any of the physical stuff. If it's a pup that I want, I'll just try it and see what happens. The way it looks doesn't make a difference.

How do you raise your puppies?

Every pup is raised in the kitchen, and it'll stay in the kitchen until it either outgrows the puppy crate that I have in there or starts working and gets dirty regularly. But my pups spend a lot of time in the kitchen as young ones, with as many little kids as I can find to play with them.

How do you usually introduce your puppies to sheep for the first time?

I usually can't wait to see what a pup's thinking. I tend to take them out with me when I work an older dog, and I'll just let them run around at my feet, or sniff the ground, or whatever, so I can see what they do when they start to show an interest in the sheep. Once they start chasing or joining in for a little fun by following the older dog around when the sheep get close, I'll put them up, and I won't take them to sheep anymore. When I start them will depend on the time of year—if it's hot, I might not get going on with the pup until fall. But I usually like to get started with a pup at around six months, if I can do that.

How about when you get serious about training the pup? How do you start your pups out in formal training?

Once they're ready to train, I bring them out on their own, without any other dog, in a controlled area. I'll usually start with about eight bigger lambs—I like to use lambs because they won't turn on a puppy the way a ewe might if she got a little fed up. So I'll put any lambs that I think are really safe for a puppy to work in a pretty good-sized corral and go in with the pup and see what happens.

Do you always start in the corral?

Not always—it depends on the pup and the situation. If the pup belongs to someone else I'll always start in a smaller space, because I don't know the pup well and I want to be able to catch him. But with my pups, I'll normally start out in the bigger field with an older dog and just have the older dog holding the sheep in close. I prefer to be out in the big field, if possible. But if I have a pup who might be a little timid, or who does a lot of diving and chasing, then I'll go to the small area. It can be hard with the Cheviot-type sheep that I have for another dog to hold them up close enough, since they always want to break away. But on the whole, I think the Cheviots that I use are good for training pups—they move, and they don't tend to turn on pups the way other breeds of sheep do. They give the pup a lot of action—there's a lot of movement and a lot for the puppy to do and to think about, and that's what I like to see.

What do you like to see in a pup's first few sessions on sheep?

I like a good tail—that's very important to me, how well they carry their tail. I also like a pup that will balance up to you easily—that's what I really look for and really like. Distance isn't really that important to me, at least at first. I'm afraid of puppies that are too wide, because I worry about what that pup will end up being later on in life.

Are there any dogs that you've trained that really stand out in your mind as having been exceptionally easy to train?

It would really have to be Pride; she was just so natural, and everything she did was just so perfect-looking. But of course, when I started with her I didn't know anything about training dogs. But she was extremely easy for me to train even so.

So Pride was obviously a dog who showed early promise and remained good all the way through.

She did. She had a good tail, a good mind, and she balanced up immediately. She was a year old before I started her, at a clinic with Jack Knox. I had no clue at all what I was doing— the most I had ever done was watch some dogs at a dairy farm. But she was always balanced just right. So I look for what she had to this day—I've never found it again, and I probably never will.

What exactly do you mean by "good tail"?

I don't like a lot of tension in the tail—I like a tail with a nice low set. The carriage of the tail has to be down, since it says a lot about the pup's mind. Dogs with a lot of tension on sheep will carry their tails really tensely, maybe straight out instead of curved.

Tell me about how you teach the stop: how and when do you go about introducing it?

All my puppies start in the kitchen, and they get all the basic obedience commands as little ones: they'll come when they're called for treats, and I'll also teach them to sit and lie down.

So they learn the words "lie down" before they're on sheep?

Yes. I do it that way because they're easier to live with in the house when they have some commands on them. They also learn to please me at a very young age. But pups that haven't been raised by me often don't have that lie down command at such a young age. With those pups, I'll just block them from the sheep (from one side and then from the other) while we're out working, and I'll tell them to lie down when I get them to stop. I'll immediately let them go again. It doesn't take many repetitions for them to understand what I want, and because I'm quick to let them get back to the sheep they're happier to give it to me.

When do you start to insist on a lie down in the working context? Do you ask for it from the very beginning, or does it come later?

It depends on how the dog itself handles the stock, and on whether or not you really *need* to ask that dog to lie down. Some dogs might have a lot of eye, and you'd rarely want to ask those dogs to lie down—you'd want to try to keep things flowing.

How do you go about lengthening and shaping the outrun?

Very gradually. Usually I move from having the dog circle the sheep to giving a little more distance. If the sheep are up a hill, it's nicer, because the dog will tend to give a little more room going up a hill, even if they're a little excited. So I'll usually try to set up little outrun going up a hill, to take advantage of that, when I decide that it's time to lengthen the pup's outrun a bit. If I've been doing some wearing I'll make sure to land at the bottom of a hill, and I'll keep the pup with me while the sheep drift up (as they tend to do naturally) to set up the outrun. I'll let the pup run out a little farther going up the hill than I would on the flat, or certainly more than I would going down the hill.

Do you pay a lot of attention to shaping the top of the outrun?

Yes, that's a very important part of training for me. A lot of it goes back to the early circling that I do with the dog, making sure that the dog gives the correct distance there. With young pups, you have to let them just bring the sheep to you at first, even if they're a little bit tight at the top. But if they gear themselves down a little bit, I'll let any tightness at the top go for a long time, because I believe that they'll fix it on their own, and if they do, it'll be fixed forever. I like them to figure out what they're supposed to be doing at the top on their own—I don't want it to be a mechanical thing.

Could you explain your basic training progression? What do you like the dog to master first, before you both can move on to the next stage?

I definitely start with the gather: they have to be gathering well before we move on to anything else. I don't mean that the dog has to be doing a *perfect* gather—you can't expect perfection out of a young dog. But if I get the dog going nicely around fifteen or twenty sheep, then I might start pulling the dog through the sheep to me, and starting the drive that way. So the dog kind of sheds off the sheep, and we learn to drive them away like that. If a dog can't take that shed, I'll have the dog bring the sheep to me, and then I'll turn around with the dog, and we'll start the drive away from me like that. But I prefer to have the dog come through the sheep to start the drive because it's good for learning shedding later—I think shedding is a good thing for dogs to do quite early in their training. It's something that helps the dog make sense of what you're asking him to do: calling your dog through the sheep to start the drive gives purpose to both the shed *and* the drive.

When do you start insisting that the dog start to be absolutely obedient to what you're asking him to do?

Once I know that the dog really, truly understands what I'm asking, then I'm asking for obedience right then and there. If I ask for a lie down and they know what lie down means, and if it's where you'd expect a dog to lie down (I wouldn't try a lie down that I knew I wasn't going to be able to get with a young dog), by golly I want them to do it. If I feel they know their flanks, I'll stop them from taking a wrong one and then ask them again in a nice way, and hopefully they'll take it.

How do you handle pups who might want to grip the sheep?

At first I don't worry much about the grip; it's usually a fear issue, and, if so, I'll let it go for awhile. If it doesn't seem to be leaving him, I'll pack a stall full of sheep, as many of them as I can get in, and I'll put the pup in there with all those sheep. I'll let them get up close and personal to the sheep that way, so they can start to feel a little more comfortable with being near them. I do a lot of pulling the dog through the sheep in that little stall, to help them get comfortable. You're not in there to upset them in any way, so you'd never fuss at them much—I just might say their name. Once they get comfortable and gain confidence, a lot of that gripping behavior just disappears.

What do you think is the easiest type of dog to train, especially for a novice trainer? What do you think is the most difficult type of dog to train?

To me, a natural dog is definitely the easiest type of dog to train. You might have some difficulties calling it off on inside flanks if it's really natural, getting those drives going, but I don't think you can beat a natural dog. It helps me, because I might not be as quick or as good a handler as one who might do better with a more loose-eyed dog—I need a dog that's going to come in at the right spot. But then you need to be careful and not get a dog with too much eye; a dog like that can be a difficult dog to train, even though it tends to be slower, which can help novices out in the beginning. But later down the road, things are going to be more difficult with a dog like that. A really speedy dog that doesn't have any eye at all isn't going to get to the right place, so a handler who's new to all this, who doesn't understand livestock and where the dog needs to be, is always going to be a couple of steps behind the action. A loose-eyed dog who doesn't feel where he needs to be is a difficult sort of dog to train, especially for a new trainer lacking in stock sense.

When do you like to start entering the new dogs that you're bringing along in trials? What do you hope to get out of those first trials that you enter?

I like to get a Nursery dog out when they're quite young. I enjoy the young dogs more than anything, so I really like getting out there with them. I don't expect a lot from my dogs in these early trials. If they get out there, try, and don't blow up or lose it, then I feel pretty good about them. I might take a dog to a trial I happen to be going to even if I'm not sure that the dog is ready yet.

When do you like to have a dog ready for Open?

It depends on how many Open dogs I happen to be running. It's hard to give a specific age, but in general I'd like to have a dog ready for Open by the time it was three years old.

What's the most important tip you'd like to pass on to people interested in starting to train a puppy for stock work?

I think raising puppies properly is a very important thing—I think if people raise their puppies correctly, don't baby them to death, teach them what a correction is and how to handle it, things will be much easier later. You need a relationship with your dog for training: it helps to love your dog, but you also need to teach your dog to respect you. A lot of novice people love their first dogs, and that's great, but some of those pups might never learn to respect them, and that's a wrong move. You really need the dog's respect for training.

Kathy Knox

BUTLER, MISSOURI

A successful border collie trainer and trialer, Kathy Knox was the 1995 USBCHA/ ABCA national Finals champion with her dog Ettrick Bob and was the reserve champion in 2005 with her Jake. Kathy has also won the prestigious Meeker Sheepdog trial, along with many other competitions around the country. She spends much of her time conducting training clinics and is widely considered one of the most popular and effective instructors in the United States.

"To me, if you don't keep the sheep in consideration, if you just stand in the middle of the sheep and force the dog out, you're taking the sheep away from the dog."

Let's start with a short bio. How long have you been involved in sheepdog training and trialing? How did your involvement come about?

I actually went to work for my husband, Jack—I think it was in the fall of 1982. I just went to take care of his dogs while he was on the road.

Had you had any experience with dogs or sheep before that?

No, not with border collies. I had a German Shepherd that I had trialed in AKC obedience, so I was kind of going that route. But I had never seen a border collie work or anything until I went to work for Jack. That's kind of where it all started. He asked me one day if I wanted to learn how to train them, and, of course, as soon as I saw how they worked I lost all interest in obedience training. So I took the opportunity and started to learn how to train through Jack and working some young dogs for him. And it all kind of went on from there.

How long a period was that?

Well, we got married in 1984, so I pretty much started keeping my own dogs in '84 or '85.

Do you take dogs in for training now, or are most of the dogs that you are starting your own prospective sheepdogs for your own needs?

They are for my own needs. We don't take dogs in at all anymore. We're just too busy on the road. If you do that, you always feel that if you're taking in dogs for training you need to work those first, so your own dogs sit. So we just don't take them in at all anymore.

How many dogs do you start a year?

I probably start about four a year. I say four a year, but it may be closer to two a year. It just kind of depends, some years I don't keep that many pups and other years I may end up keeping more than I actually really wanted to. So I would say between two and four a year.

Mostly pups that you've bred?

Yes. Every now and again we will buy a pup in, you know, just to get a different line into the kennel. Basically, a lot of times we keep our own because we want to see how our own breeding program is going.

Do you take stud puppies back?

Yes, we take stud pups back sometimes, depending on the female. Yes, we do some of that.

What do you consider the ideal age for starting a dog?

For me, I like to start mine at about ten months old. I know that some people like to start them a lot younger than that, but I just feel like maturity-wise, mind-wise, and all of that, they are just more solid at ten months. I don't like to put a lot of pressure on a young dog, and so I don't really ever know what I have until they are around ten months anyway. And even then, they can change so much in the course of training that I feel like I never try to judge a young dog until I have actually quite a bit on it.

What do you mean by "quite a bit on it"?

I'd like to have a pretty solid start. I would like it to be able to outrun maybe 50 to 100 yards. I want to see how it is going to handle the pressure of sheep. I'd like to be able to see it fetching. The thing I've found is that you can get one that looks really, really promising, and then when you start adding different training pressures to it, upping the training pressure as it progresses, sometimes you see things that you didn't see when it first started out. Or if you start taking it to different places to work it, you can see there are just so many different things that come into it. I never really put an assessment on a young dog right from the get go. It takes me quite a while to really make up my mind, "Is this dog going to make it or not?" I may give it too much time sometimes, but I feel like I'd rather lean toward giving it too much time than to give up on one too quickly and regret that

Is there an age that you think that a dog is just too old to get started?

Depending on what the dog is doing, sometimes. If it is a really aggressive, grippy dog, and maybe it is the student's first dog that they've had or they just don't have much experience, that can be a problem. We run into quite a lot of people that only see sheep either at clinics, or that have to go to someone else's place to work their dogs on sheep once a week. In those cases, I might tend to steer them to something that would be easier for them. And if someone in that scenario had a young pup that needed training, I might suggest that they send it somewhere to get a good start on it. Or if I could see that an older dog has what I would call a nerve in it, that it just can't handle the pressure of training —you can sometime just tell that it is not in a dog to be a trial dog, even at a brief clinic—then I generally tend to tell people that it just depends on their time. If they want to put the time into this dog, then go for it, but there may be another dog out there that you could find that you put in half the time and see results much faster.

What do you look for when you are choosing a puppy? What do you consider the ideal pup?

I actually don't have any specific thing that I look for other than whether or not the pup grabs me. If I look at a litter of puppies, and I just keep going back to one particular pup, if it just always draws me to it, that is the pup that I take. It doesn't matter if it is the boldest pup in the litter, or the shyest puppy in the litter, if there is just something that keeps drawing me to that puppy. I like one that wants to look you right in the eye. I like one that seems inquisitive about you, one that is trying to connect with you, one that you can see thinking. I like a pup like that. I have kept the shyest puppy in the litter because I feel a little sorry for it. And generally most people always seem to stay away from the shy pup. I have found that a lot of times as soon as the littermates leave it is all of a sudden quite bold. It is not the shy one anymore, but maybe it was the least aggressive one in the litter so it always kind of got shoved aside.

Is there any physical type that you tend to prefer?

Not really. I suppose that I don't particularly like a really fine-boned one; I like a dog with nice bone and everything And I don't mean the runt, because sometimes the runt can turn out to be the biggest one. I mean if you can just see that it is going to be very fine-boned, it maybe wouldn't attract me quite the same. Having said that, again, if we go back to the connection thing, if it just keeps seeking me out I'm not going to write it off just because of its bone either. I tend to not care for *a lot* of white, but I wouldn't refuse to take a puppy just because of something like that.
How are your puppies raised? Are they in the house or in the kennel?

They are pretty much in the kennel. When they are little and they are able to start following me, I let them stay with me the whole time I'm out. If I go out and work my dogs and the puppy can toddle along, I'll let them toddle along. A lot of times it will just fall asleep at my feet while I'm working different dogs—I'm talking out in a field now, I'm not talking a round pen or anything. The only down side to that is that it does tend to turn them on more quickly. They can be there just sleeping one day, and the next day the sheep can run past them and that can be enough to trigger their instinct and off they go.

Why do you see that as a down side? When do you like your pups to show an interest in sheep?

Well, I'm on the road a lot and usually I have too many dogs, so I would just as soon not start one until ten months or so. If I get one started showing an interest at four months and then I have to start putting some corrections on it to keep it from getting into sheep all the time, sometimes that is kind of a down side. It would be easier all the way around if it doesn't actually want to start until I'm ready to start it.

So you don't see any benefit to a dog that starts to turn on that much before ten months?

Not for me personally, because I'm probably not going to do much with the instinct until I'm ready to start it. And sometimes the stuff that you see in them at four or five months old might not be apparent again until much later down the road. I used to get all excited about a pup that started at four months and just looked really, really good, but I've learned through experience that you need to keep your judgment back until you've actually put some training on it. I like my pups with me, and that is why I tend to let them follow me around outside. Since I don't have them in the house, I want them to be with me as much as possible.

So they follow you around until the point when they turn on and then you have to put them up?

Right. And sometimes that is quite awhile. I can get away with letting them do that for quite a long time, and other times within two or three times of doing that the pup is just wanting to get at the sheep. So it just kind of depends on the individual. I think the up side to the way I do it is that the pups become accustomed to sheep and they are never really afraid of them. They are quite used to sheep running past them, sometimes jumping over the top of them. They also get used to me training dogs, so they hear a lot of different tones, a lot of times I'll be working with a pup sleeping at my feet and I'll say "that'll do" to the dogs that I'm working and the pup will just get up and follow us out. Just hearing the different tones that way, they start to pick up on things.

Do you think that it makes them more relaxed around the sheep?

Yes, because they know that it is a part of their life; it's not just something that they are going to see only once a week and then that's it. Yes, to me it takes a lot of the tension out of them.

What sort of sheep do you like to start your pups on? How many do you like to use?

Well, we're in a fortunate position in that we can start with whatever number we want. But I would say that you don't want so many that the pup is splitting them off and doing all that, so I would say maybe five or six might be ideal. I would tend to stay away from three if possible, because it makes the sheep more nervous, but a handful, five or six, even ten, whatever, something that is not so overwhelming for the pup. We generally use our yearlings because we don't breed them until they are coming two-year-olds, so that whole first year they earn their keep by working dogs. We wean them at about three months, but we basically don't work young lambs until they are seven to nine months old. We'll use them for young dogs by the time they are nine to ten months, and then right up until they are a year and a half. It works out well because those lambs don't really challenge the dogs that much but at the same time they are kind of heavy, so the young dogs have to use their eye the right way to get them to move right. If the lambs are too young to work we might use cull ewes that are cut out to go to market in a separate field. The cull ewes might be five or six years old. So it just depends on what we've got going at the time.

What size field do you like to use for starting a pup? Do you ever use a round pen?

Yes, generally we do use a round pen for starting a dog, especially at clinics. Here at home with our own pups, a lot of times we don't have to. It depends on the dog. If you can tell that the pup has got some natural balance and is not going to be real hard to get it around its sheep, we'll just start out in a field, and that field can be any size. If we're in a 40-acre field, of course, we start with the sheep just right at us.

Do you ever use a fully-trained dog to help by doing the perimeter work?

Not a lot. I feel like if I had to do that then I'd go to the round pen. Because I feel like if you do that you're just trying to keep sheep on the field, and that's just a no-win situation for anybody. So I'd just get going in the round pen, and our round pen is actually bigger than what we recommend for people. We usually say sixty to seventy feet in diameter, not much bigger than that. And you don't want to go any smaller than sixty feet in diameter.

Why don't you like to use an older dog? Do you feel that it inhibits the pup or confuses the older dog?

I don't know that it confuses the older dog as much. The way that I train, I don't have a lot of control on the puppy, no "lie down" at all. If the sheep are getting away and the pup is pretty far out where I can't get to it, I can't yell "lie down" and then send my other dog. You know, the pup would still go. So I would just as soon not have that scenario. I would rather get my control through a round pen than through an older dog. It is just very, very seldom that I would ever use an older dog in that situation. Maybe the only time I would is if sheep started to fight a young dog, then I might bring another one out to help build some confidence in the pup. But even in that situation, I would probably move in and help the pup myself first.

Are there any aids that you generally use, like a whip, a pvc pole, something like that?

Not generally. If I need to and I happen to have a bottle of water, I might slap the water bottle against my hand, or I might take my hat off, or if I have a jacket on I might flap it at the dog to kind of get it to bend out a little bit, but as far as anything specific that I use every time, no I don't have anything like that.

What do you like to see in a pup's first few sessions? What might tell you that a pup is a good prospect? What might warn you of later problems?

I like to see a little devil in them. When I say a little devil, I like to see them keen and wanting to get on with the job. If they happen to bust through the middle of the sheep on their first attempt, none of that bothers me. To me, that's just a young dog that is excited. They don't have to just naturally go out around and all that for me for me to really like them. If I can tell in its first initial approach, you can see method coming out, that's all I really need to see.

What do you mean by "method"?

Like as we walk into the field and it sees the sheep and it drops its head, you can just see it is trying to pick up the balance point right from where it is, and by doing that it might walk straight into the sheep, but you can tell that it is just trying to find the balance point. I like that kind of stuff. If it allows me to go ahead and help it get around the sheep, and if it takes pressure pretty easily without a lot of fight, and you can tell that it understands what you are asking it because it is reading the sheep itself, I like to see all of those kinds of things. I like one that will take a correction without getting real offended by it. When I say correction, I mean generally verbally, but if I have to flap a jacket or whatever at it, it'll just respond to that without getting sulky or turning off. I just like to see one that you can tell is wanting to work with you.

What might warn you of later problems? Is there something that you just don't like to see in the first few sessions?

If I see one that just automatically goes real wide and right around to the balance point and comes on like a trained Open dog. I *used* to think that that was just "wow." I'm not saying that it doesn't still wow me, but I do kind of wonder sometimes, when you see all that and it is almost like perfection from the get go, you might not have enough in it when it comes time to put training on it. You'd have to be pretty careful about how you are going to do your training from that point on, as far as I'm concerned. Because generally when you start one you are trying to *get* to that point. You are trying to get good flanks, trying to get it to pace down to sheep in the right way. If you've got one automatically trying to do that, sometimes, depending on how you do your training, you've got nowhere to go from there. In some cases with some dogs, it feels like you are always saying "C'mon, c'mon, c'mon," trying to get it to get up and actually show a little bit more devil in a way. Some dogs—I'm not saying that they are all that way—that start that way can be a little bit weak. They are not sending a message from their eye to the stock that says, "You better get moving or else." Of course, I wouldn't just write one off when I saw it doing that, but I would always question a little bit. I like the ones that seek out that natural pressure point and natural distance on their own, but when I see them doing that I like them to do it with a lot of authority and a lot of confidence.

What was the pup that you trained that you think showed the most early promise of any of your dogs when you started it? Did that dog end up being as promising as it started out?

A lot of people won't know this dog because it was back in the early days, but I had a female named Jess that I used to run. She was a daughter of the very first dog that I ever ran named Scott. She was just promising right from the get go. In fact, Jack was forever trying to get her away from me. I think if I had her now, she would have been even better. She was good, but my lack of experience at the time in training her—and I never allowed Jack ever to touch any of my dogs for training because I wanted to do it myself and I was pretty stubborn about it—held us back. So had she had someone experienced like Jack, she probably would have gone on to do a lot greater things than she and I did together, but I learned so much from her that I wouldn't trade that. I mean, she did really well. She was third and fifth at the National Finals—third at the one in Texas, fifth at the one in Sheridan, Wyoming. It wasn't like she was a slouch, but I just know that it was my lack of experience that kept her from being even better.

At what age, or after what amount of time in training, would you give up on a pup that wasn't progressing satisfactorily? How much time would you give a pup?

Well, I generally, like I said, start them at about ten months. Because I start them later, I probably give them until they are at least two. And then with my schedule the way it is, sometimes I have to give them that extra time because I'm not home enough to put consistent training on them. So I make myself not judge my young dogs with regard to other people's young dogs. Because I'm not able to get out there and give them consistent training all the time that other dogs are getting. So I tend to give them loads of time. If I feel that by the time a dog is four it's solid and ready to run, then I go ahead and run. But I don't look for consistency, I don't look for much, before age four. I know some people think that that is crazy, but that's the way that I prefer to do it.

Can you talk a little bit about the progression of training phases in your training program? What skill do you like to start with? What do you like to have them master before they move on to a new skill? What are the general phases that you use?

I like them to be in control of themselves because they understand the pressure of the livestock, so I progress in that manner. I start them out just kind of circling and trying to get them to get to the pressure point. Once I can tell that they are getting there, not just because I'm correcting them, but because they are seeking it, then I move on to the next phase in the progression. I'll start them out just at hand, then I might just have the sheep set out just a little bit farther and start to do little outruns. If I can tell that they are just really reading the pressure point the right way, I'll go ahead and try to start them on driving a little bit. And when I say driving, now none of this is the formal driving where you can actually take the sheep and drive them anywhere, because they don't have their sides or a lie down at this point, but they do understand the pressure point of sheep. So they will hold themselves in position or they will allow me to hold them there.

So how do you go about introducing that level of driving, what are you doing at that point? Are you turning fetches into drives?

I just bring them right down around me. Like I'm turning the post, I'll bring them right down around me and I try to keep the dog in the pressure point.

By moving yourself?

By moving the dog, generally.

And you do that with your body because the dog doesn't know flanks at that point?

Right. I can get the dog to stop long enough so that the sheep start to go around me. Then as the sheep go around I can stop it again so that now it's on the pressure point to start a drive. If it'll take those sheep and just drive them out in front of me only twenty or twenty-five yards, I'll call that good. To me, that is starting the basics of a drive, and I'll just keep building on it from there.

So are you lengthening the outrun at the same time that you are lengthening the drive, simultaneously?

Yes.

So you're introducing both things pretty early?

Yes. I used to not do that. I used to get everything pretty solid on the gather before I would start driving, but I found that sometimes made it harder to go ahead and start a drive.

Harder in what way?

They've got the heading instinct; they want to do it so badly anyway. It just kind of further encourages the idea that that is all you want. And, of course, some young dogs are just going to want naturally to drive because of the kind of eye they have. It just all depends on the type of eye of the dog that I'm working with. If I can tell driving is going to come really easily but that maybe it is stopping short on its outrun because of its eye and not covering right, then I won't introduce the drive as quickly.

Do you tend to prefer the dogs that like to drive more naturally, or the dogs for whom driving comes less easily?

I tend to get along better with the one that doesn't have that natural drive in it. For me, when they have that kind of natural drive tendency, they have the kind of eye that wants to kind of hold them up in some areas, like they might not cover one hundred percent. That's the sort of thing that I might pick too much at, and then I make a dog like that even worse. I tend to like one that is fairly natural on its outrun. I don't want one that is going to go too wide, but I want one that knows it can get around to the pressure point without drawing up and stopping part way around. Those dogs though are a little bit harder to get to drive because they are forever seeking that, so with those types of dogs I'll try to start to get them to drive a little bit quicker. To me the ideal would be something in between—and I've got a young one right now that's that way, she's got just the right amount. She's a pretty natural gatherer, but she's got enough eye in her that learning to drive was very easy for her.

How do you go about introducing the stop? You've already said that you don't teach the stop off stock, but how and when do you teach it?

Sometimes if the dog is really, really resistant, I'll do it off stock. All I do is this: I'll just keep blocking the dog. I start to ask for a stop when I can tell that they are reading the pressure point the right way and they are kind of holding themselves at a distance, when I feel like they are going to come into the pressure too hard, I'll start to ask them to lie down. And a lot of times because they are feeling it the right way because the distance is right, they'll just go ahead and lie down. They don't know what lie down means, but maybe because of the tone in which I'm saying it, and maybe because of my body posturing, and because of what the pressure point is telling them, they'll drop or they'll stop and stand on their feet, but they'll stop. If the distance isn't right, I don't even try to stop them. I get my distance right first and then the stop comes a whole lot easier.

What about the steady? Is that something that you are doing before you are doing the stop? Are you telling them to steady? Are you working on pace at that point?

Yes, generally because I'm working through the pressure point. It is not that I want the trial kind of steady. If the sheep are trotting and the dog is trotting, but the dog is on the pressure point, then I'll let them trot. But if I can tell that the dog is going to shove into the pressure point and make the sheep run, I try to hold them there. So I'll say "hey!" or "there now," or something like that, to get them to hold right on that precise pressure point. And once they start to feel that, that's when the stop starts to come more easily. When they hear me say "hey," they'll draw up even more each time because they feel it.

So you're getting the dog to feel the pace and treat the sheep nicely before you worry about actually stopping him?

Right. Because I want the dog's control to come because of understanding the sheep, not just because I'm telling him to lie down.

How do you go about shaping and lengthening an outrun?

Again, it all has to do with the pressure of the sheep. If I feel that at a certain distance, say at fifty yards, I can tell that the dog is really seeking out the pressure point the right way, if it starts on its outrun, it looks in, and then it kicks itself out, and it does that the whole way out on that outrun, and, also, that once it gets up to that top end (now I'm not saying that it needs to stop; it doesn't need to be perfect), but if it gets up there and you can tell that it hits the pressure point and then comes onto it, I'll generally start to gradually increase that distance then, because I know that the dog is understanding the pressure point and the sheep. If I can tell that it just gets out there and basically falls into chase mode, then I'm not going to lengthen that for quite awhile until I can get it to understand the pressure point.

When do you start to insist on absolute obedience in your commands? Can you talk a little about how you balance obedience with developing a pup's initiative and confidence?

I demand obedience on the call-off right from the get go. That is just one thing I require. I don't like to have a pup go in, while I'm trying to shut a gate or whatever, and chase sheep everywhere. And, of course, I don't have a rope or leash or anything on my pup, so when I go in to start working him, he's going to want to go to the sheep. So as I'm shutting the gate, I'll be saying the whole time, "Hey, that'll do." And if it takes off on me, I get the gate shut and I then I get across there and I just keep blocking it until I get it off the sheep. Now, again, my pups know what a correction is and they know what "that'll do" means. I start on that from the time they are puppies. They know what a correction is, they know to come when they are called, they know what "that'll do" means. But of course, instinct can take over.

So if they are running wildly around what do you do? How do you get them to come off?

I get in there and I block them. I get between them and the sheep. I try to get the sheep up against a fence—and that's why a round pen is really helpful for this sort of situation—and I just keep blocking them until I get their attention to me. And, generally, with mine that isn't too hard because they already have a lot of that instilled. I just have to break through the instinct and get them to actually hear what I'm saying. It's like, "Oh, yeah, she's in the picture." Now at clinics, it's a little different. Some of these dogs have been programmed, only because of the lack of experience of their owners, that as soon as that leash comes off it's a free-for-all. And, unfortunately, just through lack of experience, the owners go ahead and start working from that point. And that just further instills in that dog, "Okay, well, this is my five minutes," or whatever. And so generally at clinics I have to go and try to get those dogs to change and to realize that there are two of you in that picture. To me, your respect, everything, just starts right from that. I've seen quite a few dogs that, as soon as that first initial break off for the sheep is over with, the owner can get some form of control, but to me that is not true control. If your dog starts out on its own and you can't call it back, then you aren't running the show. So, that's the very first thing that I do demand: they have to come off when they are called.

What about obedience to other things—the flanks, the lie down?

Once I know that they really understand the pressure point, then I'll start putting sides on, I'll start wanting that stop, I'll start demanding more obedience.

So when you are saying pressure point, you mean when you are sure that the dog understands what balance is and how to find balance on its own?

Right. And, also, controls itself through the pressure point. Like it's not going to bust in through the middle of the sheep, it just always tries to bring the sheep to you through the pressure point. I'm always asking a dog to use its eye when it works sheep. If I see a lot of unnecessary flipping back and forth, the dog is using its body and not its eye. So that is where I'll step in, and every time it goes to flip when it is not necessary, I'll correct it. So, once I can tell that it gets in that pressure point (say it's on a fetch and the sheep are pulling off to the right, and the dog automatically goes over there and just gets on that side and pretty much stays there, and it doesn't ever flip back off), I feel like it is beginning to understand that this is the spot that it need to be to get these sheep to come straight.

So you don't really want a loose-eyed dog, you want one that uses its eye correctly?

Yes. I don't mind a loose-eyed dog if it will allow me to help it to use its eye better. But if it is so loose that you have almost to put a mechanical down on it to get it even to stay on the pressure point, I don't care for that.

What do you do with pups who want to grip? How do you handle that? Do you correct it, do you let it go for awhile?

Generally, grips come out because dogs don't understand balance, and maybe they are a little afraid. So I'll assess the situation and see why the dog is gripping. Is it only gripping to one side when I try to get it to go around? Is it just completely gripping though sheer excitement? Sometimes I'll look at it and decide that this pup just isn't ready to start. Its mind isn't in the game yet. I'll go ahead and put a pup like that up for a month and try it again then.

You mean if it is just being silly and grabbing wool?

Yeah, and with a few corrections it still isn't stopping. If I feel like it is going to be a huge fight to get through to it, I'll go ahead and put that one up for about a little bit. But if I feel like it is gripping because it feels like it can't get to the pressure point or the balance point just on one side, I'll just keep helping it to try to develop that side. I'll help it learn to get to that balance point. But I always try to recognize the reason that the dog is gripping.

How early do you introduce shedding? How do you go about it?

I usually try to get them a fairly good-sized number of sheep—twenty or thirty at least—and then I just start asking them to come through the middle of the sheep to me. I position myself and them, and to do all this you've got to have a stop and their distance has to be right.

At what point in your training progression is that usually? Do they know their sides?

Oh, they've probably been driving a little bit. No, they don't generally know their sides, but, again, they understand pressure points. When they do come in, they'll come seeking a pressure point. That doesn't mean that they're not going to look over their shoulder at the group that is behind them, or whatever, but as soon as they connect with the pressure point that I've asked them to turn on, they'll just go into that. They'll walk in like they are starting a drive.

What about whistles? When do you start to introduce whistles? Do you sometimes use different sets of whistles for different sorts of dog?

Yes, I generally start them on that once they have their sides so I can verbally reinforce them. Depending on the dog, if it is a kind of a slow dog that needs maybe a little excitement to get it going, I'll put a little faster whistle on it. If the dog is pretty quick already, I'll try to put a more soothing whistle on it that will hopefully calm it a little bit.

Do you do all the whistles at once, or do you start with the stop and walk up?

I start with the stop and walk up first.

At what point do you like to start entering your young dogs in trials? What do you like to get out of these early trials? How do you go about choosing the right trials for your young dog's development?

They are usually not ready for me even to begin to run them until they are probably close to three years old, only because I want them to be pretty solid on everything. I don't want them to lose confidence in trialing. So I generally wait until they are about three. I'll maybe go to a trial where I know that the sheep are manageable and the course is decent. I don't want it to be a really small course where the dog doesn't feel that it's got room to get anything done. So I look for those kinds of things. And I'm probably guilty of walking off faster than staying on. So if I feel like my dog is just over his head, I walk off. I never hesitate.

How do you feel about the Nursery program? Do you generally run your young dogs in the Nursery class?

I have only run two dogs in the Nurseries. Bob, the dog that I won the Finals with, was one. He just happened to be trained up and ready for the Nurseries; it wasn't that I set out to get him ready. And it was the same thing with the other dog. I was already competing with him in Pro-Novice, so I thought, "I'll run him in the Nurseries; it isn't going to hurt him." But I didn't set out to train him up as a Nursery dog. I feel that if I set out with that in mind I might put too much pressure on a young dog that was showing a lot of promise, and that by the time it was four or five it might burn out. That's why I don't generally tend to go for Nurseries. I want a dog that is going to be a solid partner for hopefully nine or ten years. And I guess I'm maybe not competitive enough within myself that I go that route. That's just not part of my passion with these dogs.

What is the most important tip that you would like to pass on to others who are interested in training a puppy?

Just don't be in too much of a hurry. And try to really understand what you've actually got. I find that a lot of people tend to forget what these dogs are all about, and they forget what instinct is. Instinct is going to override a lot of different things: it is going to override obedience and respect because it *is* instinct. They've been bred that way for hundreds of years, and if that instinct is really strong, it's going to override a lot of things. I think people forget that, and then they train through anger because they think it is just flat disobedience. To me, yeah maybe the dog is being disobedient in a way, but is it doing it out of sheer blowing you off, or is it doing it out of instinct? If it is doing it out of instinct, you have to correct accordingly. And that all goes back to the sheep. If you are not going to keep the sheep in the picture when you are training a young dog, then you are going to have a fight on your hands right from the beginning. Then, as far as I'm concerned, it all just turns into obedience.

What do you do about taking that instinct into consideration?

I always let the dog have the sheep. I don't stand in the middle and keep the dog off of them. I try to get the dog to find the pressure point. I do that by allowing the dog to make the mistakes, leaving them alone when they're right, and correcting them when they're wrong. I don't try to prevent a dog diving or gripping, or any of it. I'll just go ahead and I let it make its mistakes and then correct it. To me, if you don't keep the sheep in consideration, if you just stand in the middle of the sheep and force the dog out, you're taking the sheep away from the dog. When you do it that way, you don't care where the pressure point is. You're basically just asking for obedience, and when I say obedience I mean when you say "get back," or "get out," or whatever it is you tell it to do, you just want it to get off the sheep and you don't care if it finds the balance point. Whereas when you let the dog have the sheep, you are going to help it find the balance point. You are going to say to it, "Okay, go out and see if you can find this balance point, and if you can't I'm going to step in and correct you until you do."

Lyle Lad

GEORGETOWN, OHIO

Lyle Lad has trained working border collies for over twenty years. A successful trialer, Lyle has won the prestigious Bluegrass Classic Stockdog Trial three times in a row with her dog Cap, who is the only single dog with that accomplishment. She has also qualified to run in the USBCHA/ABCA National Finals for the past fifteen years, placing high both in the Open and the Nursery Finals at many of them.

"Every dog is different with how much control they're going to give you. So each relationship with a dog is a little different—some will let you control them totally, and others are dogs that you'll need to work out a deal with."

How did you get started in sheepdog training and trialing?

I've been training and running dogs for almost twenty years now. My very first border collie Corkie ended up being an Obedience dog because I didn't own sheep yet. My first exposure to the abilities of the working border collie was when I saw George Conboy doing a sheepdog demo with ducks at a dog show in Michigan. I was twenty-one years old then. I thought, "This is what I have to do—I have to do this." I had always wanted a farm—in fact, I had told my future husband that if he wanted to marry me, he had to want to live on a farm. He agreed (thinking that he'd be plowing up plants), and of course I thought of a farm as a place for animals. So nine years later, I got my sheep and my dog at the same time, a young, red, tri-colored dog from Jack Knox named Jock, a grandson of Wiston Cap. I trained him myself—he was an eight-week-old puppy when I got him. I had him in Open when he was four years old. I told Jack once that I thought if Jock had a better handler, he'd probably be a much better dog, and Jack replied that if he had a different handler, he'd probably be dead! He was a hard dog to handle, but from the time he was four, until I quit running him when he was about eleven, we made it into the top twenty at the National Finals every year except one. He was an awesome dog. If the sheep were really hard, we'd move up in the placements; if the sheep were easy, other dogs would do better. But he was a really good dog, and he taught me everything that I know.

How did you start trialing?

A friend of mine told me about Ralph Pulfer's trial, so we went there and got first or second in the novice class. The novice classes that they had then aren't like the ones we have now: I had to do a 200-yard outrun (outrun, lift, fetch, and pen), with the sheep held in a release pen. I watched the other classes and I saw that there was a lot more to be learned, so I continued to train my dog.

Are you currently taking young dogs in for training, or are most of the dogs you start for your own purposes?

I generally have between four and eight dogs in for training, and then I have my own young dogs. I probably start about twenty dogs a year.

What do you look for when you're choosing a puppy for yourself?

If it's my own breeding, a lot of times I'll just pick what's left. But I really have to like both parents a lot. For instance, I took my Jace to Ken Arrendale's Mac, because I really liked the way he felt his sheep. I like dogs that are biddable, and they have to be able to cover their sheep well. I want them to be into what I'm doing.

So basically, if you like the parents, you're happy with any pup in that litter?

That's right. But for myself, I prefer male dogs to females. Of course, I got Jace from Richard Fawcett, because he had a bitch named Fly that I really liked, and he bred it to Alf Kyme's Moss. I thought I'd like a pup out of that cross. The only pup that they had left was a bitch, so that's what I took. She and I worked out together really well because she wasn't sulky or soft—she wouldn't get upset if I yelled at her. She didn't need to be yelled at much, but if things started going bad, she'd just be able to shrug it off.

When do you like your pups to start showing an interest in sheep?

The sooner the better. I've had pups that are as young as eight weeks who want to get in and chase the sheep, and I have one now who's nine months old and isn't showing any interest yet, and that scares me. Jace was on the older side before she started working sheep, and that also got me concerned. I usually don't start training them until they're about ten or twelve months old, but I've had dogs that I started training when they were six months old, because they were just *so* bad that I couldn't keep them out of the sheep, and they had to have some training. So it really just depends on the dog.

What do you like your dogs to know before you start them on sheep?

My own dogs live in the house with me, so before their herding lessons begin I usually teach them tricks: "sit," "down," shake a paw, roll over, all kinds of stuff. I also teach them to get into their crates and to come when they're called. They hang with me, and they go to trials with me. I want them to get used to traveling, and I want them to understand people. I'm also trying to develop a relationship with them. When I speak, I want the dog to understand that I'm wanting something. I want to build a good relationship in which the dog wants to be with me more than he wants to be with the other dogs.

So you raise your puppies in the house?

Yes, they all get housebroken. There are times when I need to fly to different trials, and sometimes we have to stay in hotels. I don't let my dogs on the bed or on the furniture, but they do learn to function in the house.

Do they go out to a kennel after they've grown up?

Mostly. There are certain ones that keep staying in the house, like Cap—he stayed in the house his whole life. He was totally housebroken when he was twelve weeks old, and he's just always been that kind of a dog. Moses lives in the house, Jace is in the house. So I do have dogs in the house, but I have too many dogs to keep them all in.

What do you consider the ideal age for starting serious training on a young dog?

The dog tells me when he's ready. You can tell when they're ready, especially with a male dog. For instance, I've been real easy training Jake—he's eighteen months old, but if you look at his head you'll see he still looks like a puppy. If I'm getting a dog in for training, I want the bitches to be about twelve months old, and I want the males to be anywhere from twelve to fifteen months old.

So you think the females mature faster?

Yes. Sometimes I get a male at about thirteen or fourteen months, and their owners tell me that the dog is already working. Well, even if he's working, it doesn't really mean that he's ready for training. You can start a male dog at twelve months old, and he'll crash and burn, and he'll do a lot of things that you need to correct. But if you wait another three months, you'll see a real difference in the dog's attitude, and all of a sudden he'll train up twice as fast and you won't have all of those corrections that you would have had to have made. At that point they learn much faster, and you can train them for longer periods of time.

What tells you that the dog is finally ready to take the training pressure?

He's confident and starts thinking. For instance, I had a dog in for training who was about twelve months old. He'd go out and work really well for about five minutes. After that he'd go off sniffing along the fence, and I couldn't get him interested in the sheep. I'd work another dog and have him watch, trying to get him interested, but he wouldn't want to go back to work. I only worked that dog about three times a week for three months, and then after three months he was able to work about ten to fifteen minutes at a time. Sometimes you can even tell just by looking at the dog—if he looks like a really big puppy, he probably is. But the maturity of the dog is always in the back of my mind when I'm training a young one: you have to be really careful with your corrections. The dog might seem like he's gung ho, really blasting in, and you give one tough correction and he'll be over sitting by the fence. So I don't believe in coming down too hard on a dog when he's young. I have dogs in for training occasionally that might be three years old and have never seen sheep. Two months later they're totally trained. Then you get one that's twelve months old, and you might be out there for six months without making much progress. I'll tell people if I think a dog is too immature—I'll only get them out once or twice a week and adjust my price accordingly. When the dog is ready for real training, when he can take the pressure and the corrections, I'll start training him on a daily basis.

Do you think a dog is ever too old to start on sheep?

Old dogs can always learn new tricks, but with the amount of energy that goes into covering sheep, it could be difficult. If you were to start a dog at six, the dog might already have arthritis starting to set in. It might not be worthwhile to pay someone like me to train a dog who isn't going to be finished before it's eight years old. Then again, dogs age differently. I've had dogs that were old at eight, and other dogs that seemed young at ten. If someone is just training their first dog on their own for fun and trying to learn something from the process, then I don't think there's really any age for a dog that would really be too old.

*How do you first introduce your pups to sheep? Do you like
to have a controlled environment, or do you do something
more casual?*

Yes, I like a controlled environment, a small area with dog-
broke sheep. I usually try to keep my puppies out of the
sheep, because I don't want them getting hurt. I had a ewe
once who went after a four-month old pup and shoved him
into the ground. I try to avoid those kinds of experiences. I
might bring a four-month-old pup out with about a dozen
sheep into a smaller pen, just to see what he does. I tell people that if they want me to train their dog, I don't want their
pups working sheep at all until I've started them. I don't want
bad experiences.

Do you ever introduce your pups to stock other than sheep?

I don't have ducks or cows right now, so I don't use them to
start my pups. (I love ducks, and I feel bad when the dogs
work them!)

What sort of sheep do you like to start your dogs on?

I like to start a dog on ten or twelve really dog-broke sheep. It
doesn't matter whether they're wool or hair sheep—I just
want ones that are going to bank off the walls, that understand about a dog and will move away from it properly, without hurting the dog. I don't want sheep that are going to
crash against the fence and hurt themselves when the pup is
in the wrong place—I hate to kill sheep! We ran out of pasture last summer, so I sent the main ewe flock over to a
friend's house. I kept my lambs and about six yearlings that
knew the ropes (literally, that knew the fences). Even if the
dog was hard on them, they wouldn't crash into the fences,
they'd just keep going around—they knew that they couldn't
get through the fences, and they weren't going to break their
necks trying. So I like to have sheep like those for starting.

What size field do you use to start your pups?

For the first few sessions, I like to use my 100 x 75 foot oval-shaped pen. It's lined with wood, so the sheep can't hurt it too much. I also have a 100 x 200 foot area that I use sometimes. I like the smaller area because it saves my legs—I don't have to run around as much if the dogs are chasing the sheep or if I need to show them how to get back. If the dogs are a hundred yards away from me I can't do it. So it keeps everything more in my control, if I keep the distance short.

Do you ever use an older dog to help you with the pups?

No, I think that's a good way to hurt your older dog. And sometimes the young dog will start holding the sheep to the older dog—they become a sort of team, and then the wild instincts of the puppy can kick in. The older dog can also end up running himself to death, and it just isn't a fruitful way to train anything.

How long do you keep the puppy in the small oval pen?

Not long. As soon as I have him stopping and can call him off, we'll go out. If I can get close enough to the sheep in a big field so that I have a bit of control and the dog calls off, I'll start stretching the outrun.

Do you find that the early obedience that you've taught your pups helps when you start them on sheep?

Not really, at first—it's pretty different when the pup is on livestock. Hopefully the pup's natural tendencies are going to pull him toward balance. When I stop a dog, I'm going to be stopping him on balance at first, rather than randomly throwing stops at him—that would be unproductive, and it would go against the dog's instincts. So you start working with the dog's instincts first, and then you start to ask him to stop in other places. But it would be futile and stupid to try to stop a dog when he hasn't covered his sheep. The obedience or control starts to show as he calms down.

Are there any training aids that you like to use regularly when you start your pups?

I have a buggy whip. I might tie a plastic bag onto it. You need to be very careful when starting a pup. I go out with my bag, but sometimes a flick of my hand is enough to push a dog off. That kind of thing can be too hard on dogs who aren't border collies—if you're working a German shepherd, and he's too hard on the sheep, if you flick that bag at him just once he'll have heart failure.

So you work with breeds other than border collies?

Yes, not a lot, but I do it. With border collies, I can use the plastic bag on the end of the whip. Now and then I'll get a dog who pays absolutely no attention to that, and for those dogs I tend to use a stick.

Do you mean a white wand when you say "stick"?

No. I have a hazelnut stick, the same material that you'd use for a crook but it doesn't have a handle, and it's about hip-high. It's thin and hard but very light. I also have a bamboo stick; it makes a lot of noise which gets their attention.

What do you like best to see in a dog's first few sessions?

The first few sessions, I like to see a dog who can take a correction if he starts to come in too close and then get around his sheep properly. It might look wild, with sheep flying around and the dog diving, but there's something about the dog . . . you'll see the sheep take off and the dog tries to cover but then goes in to grab, but if I can get into the right place, the next thing you know, he'll go right around and tries to balance the sheep. Then I'm getting excited! I just sent a dog home the other day because no matter what I did, I couldn't keep it out of the livestock. I was being my very best Lyle Lad, and the dog would still beat me and get into the sheep and crash them against the fence. She had no desire to herd—all she wanted to do was to pull one down and eat it. The man who owned the dog was about seventy years old, so I knew that if I couldn't keep the dog out of the sheep, he couldn't do it either. I worked hard on that dog, thinking maybe if I tried this or tried that it would come around, but in the end I had to call him and tell him that this just wasn't the dog for him.

So that's a big red flag for you—a dog that has no desire to get to balance and just wants to take down sheep?

Right. And yet sometimes . . . I have a person who brought over her dog who was really bad at the gather, but it was just a hell of a driving dog—kept them together and took them away. So we've been working on driving, and flanking, and it's starting to do some good gathers. This is a dog that's been through rescue; it's three years old, had six homes, and nobody wanted it. It had all kinds of issues of biting people and other stuff. So there are always exceptions to the rule, but some dogs won't be any better than mediocre, even with a lot of work. So it depends on what you're looking for. I have people who come to me and want top-notch Open trial dogs. Well, for that you have to have an awesome outrun, you have to have great balance, you have to have pace, power . . . you need all those kinds of things. If I start working a pup who just wants to cut one sheep out and kill it against the fence, I have to think that this might not be the dog for something like that. I'm always looking to see if there are any good points about the dog, but sometimes there just aren't.

What pup did you train that showed the most early promise, and did that pup continue on to become an exceptional adult?

You know, I don't know. I've had quite a number of really nice young dogs that I've started. Not just mine, but other people's as well.

I guess behind that question is another: do you think dogs who show early promise in general end up being really good working dogs as adults?

I think if they're going to be good, they show it early. I haven't had too many who were really terrible and then got better.

Can you tell us a little about the progression of training phases in your program—what do you start with, and what process do you usually follow?

First, I want the dog going around the sheep. Then I want to be able to stop him, and call him off of his livestock. I want to gradually stretch out his outrun, and he has to be able to stop at the top if I tell him to do that. Then I start teaching him his flanks, and I keep stretching his outrun, asking for more and more control. But at the same time I also teach him to work sheep.

How do you go about getting that?

I make sure he can take sheep out of corners, out of barns, out of trailers. I'll work him on just a few sheep, and also on large flocks. And I make sure that he can drive a whole flock with ewes and lambs, that he really understands *how* to drive. I do all those kinds of things.

And when are you starting to introduce the drive?

Oh, it depends on the dog. Now and again I'll get a dog in for training that I feel is lacking basic balance and confidence in his gather. With a dog like that, it'll be a long time before I start driving, because I want that dog really to understand that he's supposed to get back there and bring the sheep to me. If I have a dog who's moving right along, who really understands the concept of the gather (even though we still need to keep making it longer and longer), then I'll start driving, and sometimes it comes pretty quick.

How do you go about introducing driving?

After the dog fetches the sheep to me, I walk through the sheep toward the dog. I stop and call the dog to my feet. As he comes to me, the sheep move away (this is all happening very close to the sheep). I try to get the dog to walk a few paces toward the sheep, with me at his side. That's stage one. Then pretty soon I'll just saunter toward the sheep with the dog walking beside me, so that he starts pushing the sheep a little bit. I don't let him gather at this stage. I just keep stretching the distance that he drives out, not letting him try to gather when I ask him to drive. Most people lose it here because they're not paying enough attention to the dog—you need to watch the dog really, really carefully to make sure that he's not going to flank around and gather.

So you're looking for slight indications that the dog is about to flank around?

That's right—slight indications, like a dip in his shoulder. If you see that, you tell the dog "here" to get him back toward you. I'm not using flanks at all at this point: the dog is just walking, and I want him to understand that he's supposed to push the sheep away. Then I'll call him back, and we'll set up for another outrun. I just want him to understand at this stage that driving is not gathering.

But you'll do both gathering and driving in the same lesson?

That's right. Eventually I'll start putting everything together, because I'll want to work on flanks and turns. I try to work parallel to the dog—I don't let him get too far ahead of me. To me, that's almost like another part of driving: you have the dog driving away from you, and then you have the crossdrive, with turns. I have the dog drive as far as he is able. As he slows or shows a lack of confidence, I start walking to maintain a connection with him. Maybe he can only drive 50 yards ahead of me, so I'll start walking, keeping the distance between us at 50 yards. The dog might actually end up driving 200 yards, but I'm still 50 yards away, and we drive to Point A. Then gradually I'll be 75 yards away, but we'll still drive to Point A. And then he'll be 100 yards away, and we'll go to the same Point A. It's like the "mom and tot" swimming lessons that I used to take my son to, when I'd hold his hand and we'd go into the water together. Then eventually we had just "tot" swimming—mom wasn't supposed to be there anymore, and I didn't get to hold his hand. So it's kind of the same thing here: when I'm close to the dog, I'm giving him confidence and holding his hand. Then gradually as he gains confidence I let him go take the sheep away on his own. Then I start putting turns in. I don't have to use cones, but some people like to put cones out to tell them where to go. So if we're using them we might drive to the cones and then add a little turn there.

Do you teach the dog its flanks before you start teaching driving, or do you teach flanks and driving simultaneously?

Yes, I work on them separately and together. Some dogs learn flanking really fast. I do work on their flanks coming off balance.

How do you go about perfecting the stop? First of all, do you insist on having them lie down on their belly, or do you let them stand if that's what they prefer?

At first, I always stop the dog on balance, and I insist that he lies down on his belly. That comes from my obedience background. You must be sure to work at a close distance. Be sure you have the stop close up, the gradually increase the distance you are from the dog. If a dog stops on his feet, he can end up moving too much. Eventually, if a dog is really trustworthy, I might say lie down, and if he stops on his feet, that's fine. But when I'm first teaching the stop, I ask them to lie down on their bellies.

What do you do with a dog who's really resistant to lying down?

I've never really had a battle over the lie down. I'll say "lie down," and if he just stops, I'll go over, take his collar, and push or pull him down. As soon as his elbows touch the ground I'll release him immediately, so he won't look on it as a bad thing. After awhile, I'll tell him to lie down, and he might stop. But as I start to walk toward him, he'll lie all the way down, and then I'll let him go. It just gets quicker and quicker and quicker. But of course, as you stretch the outrun, it gets harder, because everything is farther away and the dog is rewarding himself for not stopping by fetching the sheep toward you.

How do you go about shaping and stretching the outrun?

When we're doing it close up, I first make sure that the dog can get around the sheep and get behind. I don't worry too much about pushing the dog out wider because I believe that the outrun will eventually show itself. There are some dogs that just don't have an outrun in them, and I have to determine that as I go along in training. But you never really know what's in that dog. I usually compare it to the sort of soap my son had when he was young, with a dinosaur inside of it. As he washed his hands, the dinosaur would slowly emerge, but he never knew what the dinosaur was until the soap was gone. To me, that's the dog. I have this raw dog here, and I want him to go around and stop at the top. Now if I start correcting him, affecting his brain enough to push him off of the livestock from where he might want to be, I never know what I might be doing. As soon as most dogs start to think about the livestock rather than their own excited frenzy, their heads go down and they start to lean out at their shoulders, thinking about their sheep. Next thing you know, you start to see the outrun that's in the dog. So when I start a dog, I just want the dog to understand that he's not supposed to be in the middle of the sheep biting, and that he's supposed to get around to balance. I don't worry if they're too close. When the dog is able to go around consistently, I start lengthening the outrun by walking a few steps away and sending the dog. If the dog starts to turn his head in, I'll correct him. I might step toward the dog and flick my hat at him, telling him to get out (of course, at this point it's close up). As soon as the dog gives me the bend that I'm looking for, I step away and let him go again until he covers. So I'm teaching him to bend out from the sheep, and when he does that he gets rewarded by getting the sheep. So I just gradually get the outrun longer and longer with that process. You'll see the dog starting to understand about what he's supposed to be doing.

What else do you do while you're teaching the outrun?

I teach a stop and a redirect. If the dog is coming in wrong, I'll stop him, walk out to him, turn him out, and let him go. When he finally gives me what I want, I let him have his sheep. The stop and redirect means stop, and then don't go on that path anymore—go on a new path. If I have a dog who's always right on his outrun, I'll try to set it up so that the dog is going to need to make a decision whether to come in or go out. Generally, I want the dog to go out. So as soon as the dog starts to make a decision, I tell him to lie down, go out to him, turn him out, and get him to go out wide. I change my whistle or my voice. (You'd draw out the command like "W-A-A-Y to me" to get him to bend out).

When do you start trying to teach the dog the "steady" or "take time" command?

Well, I actually don't use those terms—to me, the right pace is the right way to do it, and I want to be able to speed the dog up. If the dog is rushing the sheep or chasing, I'll stop him and/or come down the field and growl at him to make sure that he gets up with a proper attitude. So from *day one*, I'm looking for that proper attitude. If the dog flies in and bites, or otherwise has a bad attitude toward the sheep, he's corrected for that. We work on attitude and pace: walk up means for the dog to come up at a steady pace.

So you're not actually teaching a command to slow the dog's pace?

That's right. I just want them to know to treat the sheep right. A lot of people who train dogs as a recreational activity don't have a real sense of how the sheep are supposed to be behaving. If you're a shepherd making a living from your sheep, or if you love your sheep and want to make sure that they're treated right, then you'll start handling your dog better, because you'll want to make sure that he treats the sheep right. So I never use a "steady" command—of course the dog is supposed to go steady! He's supposed to be handling the sheep right at all times.

Do you worry that teaching the dog to handle the sheep nicely from the beginning might take some of the push out of them later?

Well, pushing and handling the sheep nicely are two different things. Think about the dog who just saunters behind his sheep, following them. I never knock a dog down to that point. I want the dog to be able to hold the sheep together and to take them away with some purpose.

How do you handle young dogs who want to grip?

By the time a dog is gripping, you're way, way, WAY too late in your correction. By the time a dog has hold of a sheep, you're way off: you're the problem, not the dog. If I see a dog starting to come in to bite, I'll be just as hard on that dog as it's necessary in order to get the message through to him. With some that might be a flick of a hat, a crook, whatever it might happen to be. I take care of that stuff when we're in the little ring. By the time we're stretching it out, if I have any of those issues we go back into the ring to work it out.

When (if ever) do you start to insist on absolute obedience in your commands?

I want the dog to have absolute obedience, but also to think about everything on his own. It's a balancing act to get these dogs just right. There's one fellow that I know who trains dogs and gives a lot of clinics, and he expects absolute obedience from his dogs. Even if the sheep are bending the wrong way, and he says "come-bye," he expects the dog to do that. To me, the art of this whole deal is the teamwork—the dog is supposed to be able to read what's going on with the sheep and make decisions. Sometimes, for instance, you might not realize that the dog has a really hard sheep to handle when you're giving commands.

How do you instill that sense of teamwork in your dog?

As the dog gives control to me, I give him control back. For instance, my young Nursery dog doesn't like to stop at the top when it's a long distance—he's good at a hundred yards. I took him to someone else's place and sent him about four hundred yards for sheep, which is a big outrun for him. I knew that I wasn't going to have any control at the top. But I tried to blow the whistle anyway, since that's just what I do. The dog didn't lie down, but he did stop, and I considered that a gift. So I gave him back his sheep, just giving him a soft little walk up whistle. And he brought the sheep to me with a very good pace all the way down. It wasn't perfect control, but I thought that since he gave me something, I'd give him something back.

How early do you introduce whistle commands?

I start whistles when they know their voice commands. But I don't have a firm plan about it—I just do what seems right at the time. If the dog has a good stop, I'll start adding in the whistle. When the dog shows me that he really understands the verbal commands, then I'll start adding in the whistles.

What's the average amount of time that you think it takes to get a dog to a basic Pro-Novice level?

I just finished up a dog who learned everything in two months. But, starting from the point at which the dog doesn't know anything at all, it usually takes between three and five months for him to understand driving, know his flanks, and be able to do outruns of about two hundred yards.

When do you start introducing shedding?

It depends on how the dog takes to shedding. I'll start them, and some dogs pick it up really quickly. I started shedding with Jake, and then I quit, because he really loved that turn-back—with him, I'm having a little trouble with control. Every dog is different with how much control they're going to give you. So each relationship with a dog is a little different—some will let you control them totally, and others are dogs that you'll need to work out a deal with.

How do you introduce the shed to your young dogs?

I start out with a big group, make a hole, and pull them through. I make sure that they come straight to me, and if they don't, that's what we work on: making sure that they come exactly to me. Once they're coming exactly toward me I turn them toward part of the flock. I might split them, take a group a long ways away, split them again and take that group a long ways away, and so on.

So you start this when the dog is pretty comfortable with driving?

Usually they know how to drive. I'm always amazed when people tell me that they've just started their dogs and they're already doing sheds. I want the dog to understand about keeping the sheep together before I ask them to come into the sheep. So I'm not real quick to start shedding, but usually my Nursery dogs know how to shed—it's not like I'm waiting until the dogs are five years old.

When do you start to enter your young dogs in trials?

Before I enter a dog in trials I'll make sure that we've been out a lot to other places and that he can take sheep off of a spotter. When I feel like the dog is giving me a lot of control, then I might enter him.

How do you go about picking good trials for your young dogs?

There are a lot of good small trials in Kentucky, near where I live now, with nice dog-broke sheep. But the trials themselves don't really matter, because I'm always willing to leave the post if necessary. Some handlers stick to the post for the duration, but as soon as I see that I'm losing control or that the dog is losing confidence, I'll leave the post and put the sheep away.

How do you feel about the Nursery program and its effect on young dogs?

I like the Nursery program; I don't think that it's a bad thing. But I feel strongly that if I really like a dog but he's not mature enough to handle Nursery, I'm not going to put him through that. As soon as a set of panels is placed on the field, you're tempted to give the dog a million commands to make them. The dog might not be ready for that. I try to keep my voice light when I'm working the dog the way I do at home, and if the dog goes crazy we just quit. It's always important not to abuse someone else's sheep or blow your dog's mind.

What's your final piece of advice for aspiring sheepdog trainers?

If you have a well-bred dog, and you work it often and get it "kind of right" one out of every three times, the dog is going to learn. If he's well bred, he's going to have it in him, and when he finally starts doing the right thing he's going to like it. I'd also go to clinics and get lessons, but I really don't believe that people should go to clinics *all* the time. I think you should go to a clinic and then do a lot of hard work with your dog to try to figure out what's going on. Then go to another clinic, either with the same or even a different person and try again.

Beverly Lambert

HEBRON, CONNECTICUT

Beverly Lambert has been training and trialing border collies for more than twenty years. A fierce competitor, Bev has had great success on the trial field. Her impressive record includes reserve champion at the USBHCA/ABCA National Finals three times (once in 1997 with her bitch Lark, and twice in 2002 and 2006 with her Pippa). In the past few years, Bev has trialed extensively throughout the country with her dogs Pippa and Bill, winning prestigious sheepdog trials such as Meeker and Soldier Hollow on multiple occasions.

"I think people should pay more attention to the kind of dog they want to be training."

How did you start out in sheepdog training and trialing?

We had a small sheep ranch in eastern Maine, and we traded a few sheep for a dog. I had the Longton and Hart book that I used to train her, and that was my first dog.

What made you decide to get a dog?

I read *Bob, Son of Battle*. I had never seen a dog work, I just thought that it sounded like good idea that there was a biological solution to our problem.

How many sheep did you have then?

About a hundred. We had no fences, so they would just wander off. We'd go and get them with our Airedale and a motorcycle, but I figured there had to be a better way.

What kind of sheep were they?

There were a mixed commercial flock. And that was 1981.

Do you take in dogs for training, or are you starting dogs as prospective sheepdogs for your own work and trial needs?

Primarily, yes. Sometimes someone will come with something that they have bought from me that they are having trouble with, and I'll be interested enough in the breeding to want to mess with the dog. But I don't usually.

How many dogs do you start a year on average?

One or two.

What do you look for in a puppy? What do you consider the ideal pup?

I used to have a lot of things that I looked for, but the last couple of puppies I've just asked them to send me whatever sex I happened to be in the market for at the time and never even looked.

What were the things that you used to look for, and what made you give up on that?

Well, I never picked the right puppy! I don't know, I think I usually just picked them by looks: whichever one I thought was prettiest. Then I got into whichever pup was the most outgoing. Then, I don't know what I was doing. I won't mess with a pup unless it's a team player. Unless it wants to be doing what we're doing, I get rid of it real fast.

Is that something that you can tell with young puppies, I mean before you're even starting them?

No, you can't. It'll seem pretty obvious to you, like you'll have one that won't come to you when you call it in the yard and that just seems really independent. Then you get onto sheep and it'll be an easy-to-get-on-with dog, then sometimes you'll have one that is just a love bug and you'll get it onto sheep and it just doesn't have the time of day for you. So you just can't tell.

How are your puppies raised?

Well, ideally I'd raise them all in the house. They certainly all spend some time in the house, they usually sleep in the house, but I'm at work all day so they spend the day out in the kennel. It's not a great situation because they are kenneled with a lot of other dogs, so they tend to be a lot more interested in the rest of the dogs than they are in me. But that changes. As soon as you start working them, they really come around. And I've raised a lot of puppies and they start out more interested in the other dogs than they are in me because of the poor way in which I raise them, but as soon as I start training them, if they are any good at all, their whole attitude changes.

So you think the bond with you will kick into gear once you start working a pup on sheep, no matter how it's been raised?

If it is going to, yes. But some of them just aren't going to bond that way, and those are the ones that I don't mess with.

What do you like to teach a pup before you introduce them to stock? Do you teach a recall, a lie down, anything much off of stock?

They have to have a recall so that I can get them into the kennel in the morning. And then I just like sort of general kinds of discipline so that they are reasonable dogs to live with. So we take them for a lot of walks. They learn a lot of stuff because I have a pack of dogs that they run with, and so they are in the yard a lot with those dogs, and they learn from those dogs to come when they're called, not to bark a lot, sort of what is and is not allowed. So I don't like a barking dog, I don't like a dog that won't come when you call it, I like a dog that kind of looks at me when I'm talking to it, and generally a dog that is easy enough to live with. And if they are too hard to live with at that age, I don't mess with that either.

So you don't teach any sort of formal commands?

No, except a recall.

So they are just kind of running with your other dogs and learning the basic rules of your household?

Yes. They have a good recall and they have "no," they *really* understand "no," and that is the thing that I really want them to understand before I ever take them to sheep.

When do you like to see pups show an interest in sheep? Does it matter to you?

I don't care. Actually, I've gotten to the point now where I really don't want them to be too keen too young because our fences aren't good enough to keep them out of the stock. I just don't like having them in the stock all of the time. So, when we are feeding sheep and stuff like that, I'll try to always put the puppies away so they don't have the opportunity to get in there and show that kind of interest. I just don't want them starting.

How do you first introduce them to livestock? Do you just let them follow you along while you are doing chores?

No, I go out there. I take another dog. It is very controlled. Well, maybe not very controlled—I do use the whole field. But I'll bring another dog out, I'll gather up all the sheep, I'll hold them pretty close to me, and I'll let the dog pull a line and just let them go. Then I'll let them go and chase the sheep around until I can catch them.

So you do use an older dog for that?

I use an older dog to get the sheep up to me, because I can't get close enough to them with a puppy—they know what is coming.

What do you consider the ideal age to start a dog in formal training?

October.

No, seriously.

Seriously. I start them in October.

October, no matter how old they are?

They need to be at least six or seven months old. I used to start them younger, and I think it is a mistake. I used to start them as soon as they showed an interest in sheep—and you can actually get a lot on them at that age because they are so malleable and so sensitive. I think if you wait until they are a bit older, they are harder to start, harder to get going, because they are more self-confident, but if some little thing goes wrong it gives them that extra little bit of reserve to fall back on. So if they get hit by a sheep and they are six months old, it has a real impact on their psyche, it means a lot to them. If they get hit by a sheep at ten months, it doesn't mean as much to them. They are harder to train because things don't mean that much to them, but it is a lot easier not to make a mistake.

So why October?

Because that's when the trial season is over. I start in October and train through the winter.

What sort of sheep do you like to start your pups on? How many sheep do you use, and what kind of sheep?

I like to start them on something that is not going to do anything to shake their confidence. So, I just use most of my flock of school sheep.

How many is most of your flock?

Oh, about fifteen or twenty.

And you keep on with that number for awhile?

Yes. I don't like to work them on a smaller number of sheep because it encourages the development of eye, and I don't like eye in a dog. I just like enough eye in a dog for it to look good.

What do you mean by "look good"?

Set up on the sheep, show some style. But I don't like to see a lot of eye in a dog, it interferes with their ability to do what you want them to do.

What size field do you use for starting pups? Do you use a round pen?

No, I just start them out in my five or six acre field.

So you start them on five or six acres with fifteen or twenty pretty dogged sheep?

Yes.

Do you ever use stock other than sheep, ducks or goats?

No. I figure part of what they are learning at that early age is about stock. For the rest of their life, learning about goats and ducks isn't going to do them any good. I've got to spend a lot of time out there teaching them to listen, helping them to develop a work ethic, and all of that kind of stuff. So while I'm doing that, they are learning about sheep. So that is the good thing they are getting out of that—in addition to all the rest of it—you miss all of that if you are chasing a bunch of runner ducks around.

So your sheep are wool crosses at this point, or hair crosses?

Right now they are Katahdin and Barbados crosses, and then there are some wool in there. The wool sheep are Perendales.

The dog is working that whole group of wool and hair mix?

Yes, but if the puppy is too wild I'll pull the wool sheep out because they are more likely to run into me, and I don't want to be run into.

Do you ever use any aids like a whip or a pvc pole or any-thing?

Yes, I usually have my stick with me. It is as much to defend me from the sheep as it is to discipline the dog.

What do you like to see in a pup's first few sessions? What would tell you that the pup might be a good prospect? What might warn you of later problems?

Turning tail and trying to get off the field is always discouraging. I like to see them trying to come forward. I like to see them want to get to their sheep. In a perfect world, I like to see their heads come down and see them start showing some of that style that we're all looking for.

A lot of people have said that in an ideal world they would like to see a dog go smoothly behind to balance, but it seems like you're more interested in the dog coming forward. Is that right?

Yes, that's right. I don't care if it has a natural outrun. To me, the attitude of the dog and the character of the dog is more important than what it actually shows me in that early work.

Say more about that. How would you put your finger on attitude and character that you are seeing just in the beginning?

That's the tricky part, isn't it? Hmm. How would I put my finger on it? Well, that's the thing I'm looking for. I'm looking for him not to be afraid of the sheep, to want his sheep, to come toward his sheep. I'm looking for him to respond to me appropriately, so that when I say something to him he responds to it without being afraid—so he's got enough self-confidence. I'm just looking for the dog with the right character to accept the training and the discipline, and that's more important than his instinctive package of abilities.

Can you see that sort of thing from the beginning?

Yes, you can pretty much see it early. I mean, it's always impressive to see a young dog go out and cast around sheep, but all that tells you is that the young dog will cast around sheep. It doesn't tell you anything about what your final product is going to be like. Whereas a dog that puts its head down and just comes into those sheep, and wants to get to them, and is keen to work, can be even more impressive than a dog who bends out away from his sheep and goes around them. Because that dog is always going to want to get to his sheep, whereas the other dog, maybe he doesn't want to get there as badly. Sure, he's got a nice move there, but I don't like to see him giving ground to his sheep like that.

What was the pup that you trained that showed the most early promise? Did that dog end up being as promising as it started out?

I haven't had any that I thought were brilliant youngsters that haven't turned out to be nice dogs. Let me see if I can think of one. Well, Maid, the first time I took Maid out, she was a real obvious dog. You could see all of her holes and you could also see all of the good stuff about her. And the good stuff turned out to be there, and most of her holes, with age, have gotten to be lesser problems. I think that the good ones will just keep getting better.

So you think that there is a pretty strong correlation between early promise and a good dog in the end?

I think there is a good correlation between what they are like when you first start working them, and what they turn out to be. I don't think there is a good correlation between how they look when they get loose and start running around sheep at ten weeks old and how they turn out to be. I think there is almost no correlation. So when you see that cute little puppy in there with his head down and everybody thinks, "Oh, there's a world beater," I don't think that means that much.

So you think the correlation starts when they are older and ready to accept training?

Well, it does for me, of course, because of all the things I've just said that I'm looking for in a dog.

When do you give up on a dog? At what age or after what amount of time in training would you give up on a pup that you didn't think was progressing?

I don't know, I have one here that's three and I'm still beating my head against that wall! Oh, when to give up? It depends on the dog. You can tell. I know this one that I talk about beating my head against the wall, I know she's not going to amount to anything, and I've known it for quite a while, and she's got some really nice moves. If they won't listen to me, if they don't want to do it, I won't keep going out there. The dog that just gets the bit in his teeth and goes after the sheep and won't listen and doesn't learn anything, I won't keep messing with. There are people that don't mind training a dog like that, but I do this for fun. I don't do it for a living. So I don't have to work with a dog like that, he can go somewhere else where somebody has got to train him because he's doing it for a living.

So you want a dog that is showing a pretty strong interest in being a team player with you?

Absolutely, and that's why that character is so important for me, because quite often that kind of softness in a dog is related to softness about a lot of things. And so I need a dog that wants to work with me, but also wants to come forward, get his sheep, and has enough guts to work the sheep.

So you are saying softness in this context as a good thing, the way the horse people use it?

Absolutely. For me, softness is a good thing, but it has to be mixed with guts, and that is a hard combination to find often.

How do you first introduce the stop and the steady? How does pace fit into your program? How do you introduce a lie down, how do you get them to check themselves?

What I do is I take the puppy out to the stock. Once he's going around with confidence and enthusiasm, I'll start making sure that he's showing enough distance. And to me, the most important thing in all that early training is the dog's attitude toward the stock. And once I've got him so that he's showing respect for the stock, then we will start working on some of that other stuff.

So how are you going about it? You are going out there and you are just kind of having them circle and have a proper attitude, is that right?

Yeah.

And what do you do if they don't? What do you do if the dog just blasts in, scatters the stock, and isn't listening to you?

I'll step in and put pressure on him, however much pressure I need to put on him to get the right response.

So, now that you've got the dog's respect and the dog is showing a decent attitude, what do you do next?

Then you are pretty well golden and you start teaching him all of the commands for it. But by that point, he's working and you're off.

How do you go about lengthening and shaping the outrun?

I'm asking that dog to go around sheep that are close to me during all the beginning stuff while he's learning the right attitude. When he has the right attitude he understands that when he goes around sheep he needs to give them enough space. Once he understands that and is relaxed and has a nice stop, I can send him to the sheep from anywhere and he'll do it correctly.

So are you insisting at that early stage on a stop?

Fairly early on I make that dog stop; I'm not shy about asking for the stop.

Do you care if they stop on their feet or lie down, or do you let the dog choose what seems most natural?

Early on I'm pretty slack about it, but with passing time I'm more inclined to start keeping them on their feet.

So you like them on their feet?

I do.

What about steady as a command? Are you just kind of teaching them the sense of pace or are you actually teaching steady or take time as a command from early on?

I use it all the time. What it means differs with your tone of voice. It can mean that what you are doing is good and to keep on doing it. If I say it in a gruffer voice, that becomes a discipline, and it means that whatever you are doing isn't making me happy and that you should try to think of something else to do.

When, if ever, do you start to insist on absolute obedience to your commands?

Early on. Pretty early on.

How do you find you balance obedience with developing a pup's initiative and confidence in handling stuff on their own?

When dogs can give you obedience, you insist on obedience, and when they are in situations where they are feeling a little stressed and can't give you that obedience, then you just try to help them through it. So when they are at the balance point and you ask for the stop, then, by God, they better stop.

So you try to ask for things that they can do and minimize the things that they can't do in the beginning?

Yes. If some sheep is running away and some puppy is in hot pursuit in an inappropriate way, I let it go because my yelling "lie down" at him isn't going to have any impact except to diminish his responsiveness. If he's at the balance point and everything is standing there and I tell that puppy to lie down and he doesn't lie down, he just keeps walking forward, then I'll go right through the sheep at him and make him lie down. And if I've got a less confident dog, I'll let him come on more so he'll gain more confidence on his sheep. It varies. When I first go out there with them and they are a bit wound up, I don't usually ask them to stop. I introduce the stop later in their training. But when I do ask them to stop, I make sure it is in a place where they can stop and where I'm in a position to make sure that they do.

How and when do you first introduce the drive?

Very early on. I get them going around sheep and then I pretty much ask them to drive them away, probably before they have an outrun.

So you're not doing a whole lot of wearing?

I hardly do any wearing. It's so boring. And again, I don't feel that it teaches them anything worthwhile to anything else that's going to happen in their careers.

If you had a dog that was very forward and more inclined to drive than to gather naturally, would you still introduce the drive early?

Yes, and I'd just be thankful that I had a dog that had that kind of attitude. If the dog wants to drive and isn't too good about gathering, I don't worry about it too much, because the reason we teach the gather before the drive is that most dogs naturally want to gather—it seems easier to us to teach him that first. But if a dog naturally wants to drive, teach him that first because *that* is easier for him to learn.

What are some of the most common problems that you see when you are starting new pups, and how do you handle those problems? What do you think are the top one or two biggest challenges that you've come across when you are starting new dogs?

I don't think it's that simple. I guess because of the kinds of dogs that I like to work with, the biggest problem I'm inclined to see is that the dogs don't have enough come forward. They tend to be a little bit diffident and maybe a little bit scared of the sheep. So I guess the biggest problem I have is dogs that aren't confident enough on their stock.

What do you do about that? How do you get them more confident?

I tend to let them go more. So I let them be more aggressive and then I deal with the problems that develop down the road.

What about dogs that might have a chasing problem, or a gripping or grabbing problem, how do you handle those?

The whole beginning part of my training is about the dog developing respect for the stock. He needs to learn that kind of self-control that keeps him off his stock. So if he doesn't learn that, if he just keeps chasing them and won't listen to me when I tell him to get back, I get rid of him.

And the same thing with gripping, a dog that just might blow up?

Yeah, and if he wants to do this and if he wants to learn, then he's going to go out there with me and he's going to work with me and he's going to learn. But if I go out there with him day after day after day, and he's just running in and grabbing sheep, then that dog really needs some serious discipline and I don't want to mess with it. And I'm lucky, I don't need to.

How about shedding. How early do you introduce shedding?

That is pretty late in my program, actually, because I like to get them penning really well.

How do you work on penning?

I don't do any of that stuff until they are working really well. So they've got a nice gather and they are driving really well; a good drive is really important to me. So I spend a lot of time working on that, and then when that's really good, and probably about the time I'm getting ready to start trialing, I'll take them out and we'll do a little schooling on their pen work, and that is just to make sure that they've got the right shape to their flanks when they get up to that pen.

And shedding comes after that?

Shedding I don't usually mess with until they've finished their Nursery season. I really do leave it until quite late.

And why is that? I mean, I think that some people think that if you introduce shedding that late you might not end up with a really good shedding dog.

Oh, you maybe don't, but that is just when I do it. I wait until I'm done with the season.

Is that just because you don't want to confuse anything for the Nursery trial work?

Yeah, and they're getting a lot of drilling all through that to make them really perfect before the Nurseries, and I just don't need to be out there trying to throw some other confusing thing at them.

How about whistles? When do you introduce whistles?

Pretty early on. About a week or two into their training. I just carry a whistle with me and I'll use a whistle. I've trained dogs where I never used a voice command for their flanks. I don't do that as much as I used to, because I find that I like those voice commands, that I want to be able to do that, but I used to do it that way.

Do you have a standard set that you use for all of your dogs, or do you like a different set for different sorts of dogs?

Actually what I tend to do is choose the whistle set of any dog that I just happened to have recently purchased, so that I can get those whistles into my head.

At what point do you like to start entering your young dog in trials? What do you like to get out of these early trials?

I tend to enter them as soon as I have good control on them, so I know that nothing bad is going to happen. And I like them to just get the whole thing, the whole package, being away from home and working on different sheep. The main thing that I am looking for is that they listen and that they have a good time. If either one of those things appears to be in jeopardy, I'll just retire.

How do you go about choosing the best trials for your dog's development? Are there some trials that you just think, "Oh, the sheep are terrible. I don't want my dog exposed to those sheep at this stage"? Or do you just not worry about that sort of thing?

It is usually determined by how close it is and what the entry fee is. I figure that I can control all of those things. There aren't any trials around here where the dog is going to get hurt by the sheep, so I don't have to worry about that, and if I am running and things aren't going well, I can always retire.

I gather from what you've said that you really like the USBCHA Nursery program?

I think it has been very good for dog trialing in this country. So, yeah, I do like it. I think it is fun. I think it could be better, but I think it is a good idea.

Do you see people pushing dogs along too much?

No, I really haven't. A lot of people worry about that, but I don't think it is an issue. I think the thing that happens is that a lot of dogs look really good as Nursery dogs, but there is not that much competition in the Nurseries. So you've got these brilliant young Nursery dogs and then the Open season comes around and they're not brilliant. So everybody says, "Well, he really pushed that dog along too fast because he's not that good," or "He ruined it, because it was just brilliant as a Nursery dog." Well, he was brilliant when he was competing against only dogs his own age in a very small pond. When he hit the big time, he just wasn't as brilliant. And I think that's all it is. I've had a few brilliant Nursery dogs myself, and people will ask me about a dog, you know like "Well, how good is that dog?" And I'll say, "Well, I think he's going to make a nice Nursery dog. I don't know if he'll make an Open dog." There are some nice Nursery dogs out there that are just not necessarily going to make it as Open dogs, even with top Open handlers.

What's the most important tip that you would like to pass on to others who are interested in training a puppy, maybe people training a dog for the first time?

I think you should get a dog whose parents or siblings have the qualities that you want to train in a puppy. Some people buy puppies because of the performance of the parents—and certainly performance is a nice thing to go by—but if you want to train something that needs to be hit in the head with a two by four just to get it to glance at you, there are dogs out there that will produce that. If you want to be out there with something that is a team player, there are dogs out there that will produce that. And I think people should pay more attention to the kind of dog they want to be training.

Amanda Milliken

KINGSTON, ONTARIO, CANADA

A driving force on the trial scene in the United States and Canada for the past twenty years, Amanda Milliken is one of the few handlers who exclusively trains and handles dogs from her own breeding lines. The crown to her many placements and wins in prestigious trials occurred in 2005, when Amanda and her dog Bart (the great-great-grandson of her first border collie Bart, after whom he is named) were the National Champions in the USBCHA/ ABCA National Finals in Sturgis, South Dakota.

"I am very poor about demanding absolute obedience out of a dog. But mostly I try to make sense out of the job so that the dog knows where it is headed with what we are doing."

How did you start out in sheepdogs

My sister Kathy actually got the first sheepdog in our family; I didn't know anything about them. She had been at riding school in England and had been on a farm where they had a mixed dairy/sheep farm—lots of people in Yorkshire have that. She had seen border collies working there, and she wanted to get one when she got home. She got a good one from a guy in Tennessee. It used to bring her horses in, and I just thought it was a remarkably smart dog. We had a handful of sheep, hobby sheep, and someone had dropped off a sheep that had never flocked up with the sheep before, just cattle, so it hung with the cattle at our place and we never could catch it. It had a couple of years of fleece on it—we never got it shorn because who would come and shear one sheep, and we could never catch it at shearing time, either. One day that dog was hanging around, and it had been here for maybe six months, and I said, "Put that sheep in the barn." And she did. I ran to the house and said, "Mother, we've got to get one of these dogs; she just put the cow sheep in the barn." That's how it came about, and I got my first one. His name was Bart.

So you had sheep at your farm before you had any border collies?

Yes, we had a hobby flock of about twenty-five sheep.

How many dogs do you start a year on average?

I try to train two over the winter.

Do you take in dogs for training, or are you starting dogs as prospective sheepdogs for your own work and trial needs?

I don't take in any dogs for training. I don't have time.

What do you consider the ideal age for starting a dog?

It is so variable. I think that one is kind of a good time to start.

What age, if any, would you consider too old to get started?

That is variable, too.

What do you look for in a puppy? What do you consider the ideal pup?

I don't have any expectations of puppies. I don't know what makes me pick one. I just take a shine to one and keep it. And actually Eucher was left over; nobody wanted her, and she stayed. For a long time, she was a great bitch for me. So, I don't have anything in particular that I look for. Sometimes I've had the one that has been left over and it hasn't been any worse, and sometimes it's even been a lot better. Who knows. I don't like red ones, so that's out, and I don't like them to be overly white. But red is the bottom of the barrel for me.

Have you had red pups in your litters?

Yeah, I have. Hazel had red littermates. Big, rough-coated red ones. Hazel was this little, black-and-white, smooth-coated bitch.

How are your puppies raised? House dogs, kennel dogs, some time at each?

Some time at each. I usually keep puppies in the house overnight. I crate them. They're outside during the day. I don't like them to wreck my garden, so I like to put them in a run or something. When I'm home I keep them with me, even in the garden—I teach them not to go into it.

When do you like to see pups show an interest in sheep?

I don't really care. If they show an interest before six months, well, it's kind of fun, but there's not much you can do with it. So I'm not worried about that. If they don't show an interest by the time they're a year old, I often let them go. But maybe I shouldn't, that might be premature. I just get impatient with them.

How old are your pups when you first introduce them to sheep?

Any time. If they are three months old, I'll take them with me when I walk into the barnyard or something. Or when I walk out to see the sheep, or do something with the sheep, I'll let them see. If they start to chase around after them, I start putting them away and don't let them loose.

How many sheep do you like to start a pup on?

A dozen. Ten.

Do you prefer lambs, older ewes, any mixture?

If it were a really young dog, let's say it was eight months old and not that quick, I wouldn't mind older ewes. But I dispense with that very swiftly, too. I want sheep that will run away and the dog has to learn to cast off and take care of the job, or lose them. I want them to learn that if they do certain things they will wreck everything.

So would you just end at that point? Let's say the dog just dove in and scattered the sheep all over the place, would you just call it a day?

No, I'd tie the dog up, I'd gather them back up, or try to, or get some new sheep, and try again. I don't like to end on a sour note ever. I like to do something that the dog can do at the end of every training session and be successful.

What size field do you prefer for starting a pup? Do you ever make use of a round pen?

No, I don't do that round pen scene. I like the dogs I start to learn the cause and effect of things they've done. So if the dog loses the sheep, I like the sheep to be able to *get* lost; I don't want the dog to be able to do something terrible without consequences. I like to see them get away and mayhem ensue and the dog be sorry about it. "Shoot, those sheep got away!" Maybe next time it won't cause the same damage.

Are there any aids that you make use of as a general rule, say a whip or a pvc pole?

No. I've been known to toss something at a dog that completely ignores me, but outside of that, no. Maybe in individual cases I would want it, if a dog did ignore me. But I haven't had that problem that much either.

Do you generally enlist the aid of a fully-trained dog in starting a young dog?

Yes, ride herd a little bit and get things back if they really fall apart. Most of those dogs know the job now, and they are pretty good at hanging back and watching the training.

Do you ever use a light line?

I have in cases with people that have brought dogs that are kind of unmanageable or difficult to catch.

What do you like to see in a pup's first few sessions? What would tell you that the pup might be a good prospect? What might warn you of later problems? What are red flags?

Of course, I like to see a dog that settles behind its sheep nicely and steadies up and brings them. I try to encourage them to get into that place with whatever it takes, whether it is me moving to 6:00 so it pops them down at 12:00, whatever it takes. But I don't have red flags when I first see dogs. Heck, the dog that I'm running right now that I really like, when we cut him loose for the first time he ran around barking and biting the sheep, with everybody laughing. But, boy, he settled down within a week and started looking like a smart dog. So as long as they are interested, something can be done.

What was the pup that you trained that showed the most early promise?

Hazel.

Would you say that she turned out the best of all of your dogs?

You know, maybe so. I like the dogs that I'm running right now. So it's hard to say, and they are all different. They have different things. But if I look for a pup, I always want Hazel. I always want to get her back.

Do you think you would do things differently if you did get her back, or are you happy with how you brought her along?

She was really the first dog that I trained properly. I was happy with everything she did, really. She was a great dog to run, a great dog to own.

Do you find that the dogs that come along the most easily are necessarily the best dogs in the end, or do you think that one thing has nothing to do with the other?

No, I think that one thing has nothing to do with the other. You can duke it out, sort through a dog's problems, sometimes at the end of the pike they're the better for it.

At what age or after what amount of time in training would you give up on a pup that just wasn't progressing satisfactorily?

I would say by about a year and a half I would like to see something happening. And it would depend on how much time I put into it. After two or three months of training, I sure would like to see some progress. If I hadn't, I might say adios. I have given up on ones earlier than that, too. I like to see a style of learning where they apply themselves. I hate it when you come back the next day and the dog acts as though the previous day never existed. I can't stand that. So it is a style of learning that I really dislike, and if I see that in a dog, I would prefer not to deal with it.

What, if anything, would you expect your pup to know before you introduce him to stock? Does it have a lie down, does it have a recall?

I sure would hope that it would come when it was called. To me, the lie down would just be a luxury. The lie down comes to a dog when it gets around stock because it is such a logical thing for a good dog to do when you ask for it in the right place. You say it and it's, "Oh, yeah, what a great idea. I'll do that."

What is the progression of training phases in your training program? What skill do you start with, what and when do you move on to the next skill?

I start them going left and right and give words when the dog is doing it on its own. I try to stop them at 12:00. Eventually,

I stop them at different places, not just at 12:00: 3:00, 9:00, odd spots. Then I start demanding flanks when I want them, rather than when the dog chooses to do them. I stretch that out and go for little outruns. Send the dog. Stretch them out. Have them fetching. Try to build some pliability into the fetching. Then after they are fetching well I start driving, and I walk with them a lot.

Do you turn your fetches into drives, or do you turn and have them drive in the same direction that they fetched?

Not early on. I get them around behind me and then start off on the drive with the dog and walk beside it, and then just drift farther away as the training progresses. But I try to stay within eye shot so they always think I'm going to come.

When do you first introduce the stop? You said that you try to stop the dog at 12:00 as you introduce little outruns?

Yes, right then. And it feels natural—if you get a nice young dog, you'll see it pull up at 12:00 eventually and try to hold that spot, or at least recognize it as a place where they can feel comfortable holding sheep to you. It gratifies them.

When, if ever, do you start insisting on absolute obedience in your commands? How do you balance obedience with developing a pup's initiative and naturalness and confidence?

I am very poor about demanding absolute obedience out of a dog, as probably everybody knows. But mostly I try to make sense out of the job so that the dog knows where it is headed with what we are doing. The young one I'm training now is an obedient type of dog. In my reckless training he's become less obedient than he was right off the bat, but he's pouring onto his sheep nicely, and I actually like the work that he's doing and it seems like he has enough of a stop for me.

How do you handle pups who want to grip? Do you ignore it for awhile, do you make an issue of it?

There are all kinds of reasons to allow grips, and it depends on the situation. I am not adamant about it, and I'm not even adamant about it in trials. I think some of the grips that are called off are silly. And I think people should let their dog win all of the time no matter what it takes. A dog cannot be stopped from carrying out its job, which is to have some authority over sheep. If you barge in and take the grip out of it, some measure of last resort, to me you are taking away the arsenal that the dog has got locked up, you know? I think that you should let them grip; I don't mind it. Now it's another thing to be out savaging sheep or pulling at their guts or tearing them down. I don't allow that. That has nothing to do with having authority over sheep; that is just savaging them. But I think that dogs should be allowed to grip; I don't mind it at all.

Would you put a formal grip command on a dog, whether it was inclined to grip or not? Do you teach a dog to grip as part of your regular training?

Yes, I do. Some I can't get them to grip that well, but eventually I usually can. I usually say "shift it" or "shift."

How early do you introduce shedding? What is your method for teaching the shed?

I introduce it very early on, when I'm just walking about with the sheep I've got out to train, my ten or twenty or whatever number it is. At a time when the sheep drift apart just naturally I call the dog in and turn them, hopefully on the rear ones, and take them away. But I don't break them up myself so much, I wait until there is a natural break in the sheep, and if something like that comes up I take advantage of the opportunity to teach the shed.

What about the look back? Would you introduce the look back while teaching the shed, or do you think that tends to confuse the dog?

I find that it could mess up the shed. I don't like the dog leaving the job too prematurely, anticipating turning around and going for the other ones. I send them around the sheep that I took away in the first place and put them back with the others. How do I teach a look back? I get a group of sheep, say 20. I take half. I take them away 200 yards. Then I leave them and walk away with my dog and wait for him to go for a run back to the ones I left initially. Then I send them around for the sheep that are breaking back—you've got to have your sharp timing here—I send them around the sheep that I took in the first place, the first shed off sheep, and as the dog gets behind them then I ask them to look back and pick up the other ones. But I try not to just do it when I'm initiating a shed. I don't really like that. Actually, I have overeager go-back dogs anyway.

So this is something you just might introduce in their training as a dog approaches the Open level?

No, I do it early on. And I also make it a point, because I've got over-eager going back dogs, not to train it at trial season at all. It's something that I do in the fall and then forget it. They just like it too much. They go back unasked. That's what happened to me at the National Finals in 2005. I didn't like it.

How about whistles? How early do you introduce your whistles?

When I start getting any distance at all, I want whistles. So if I'm stretching them out, I'm getting them on whistles.

Do you start with just a stop whistle and walk up whistle, or are you starting with all of the whistles at once?

All of them at once.

Do you pick an individual set for each dog, or do you put everybody on the same set?

I put everybody on the same set because I can't tolerate other whistles. I'm not swift enough at a trial. I can't manage it.

At what point do you generally like to start entering your dogs in trials? What do you want to get out of these early trials? How do you go about choosing the best trials for your dog's development?

For my first one, especially for a dog I haven't really gotten off of the farm before, I want easy sheep. I want to give the dog a happy first trial experience.

What do you think about the USBCHA Nursery program? Do you think it is beneficial to young dogs?

I do think it is beneficial. I don't think it is bad at all. Some people are going to rush young dogs whether there are Nursery trials or not.

What's the most important tip that you would like to pass on to others who are interested in training a puppy?

Be prepared to lock your dog up. Don't let it run loose once it gets interested in sheep. It is a terrible mistake. Unsupervised border collies are trouble.

Barbara Ray

MILLBORO, VIRGINIA

Barbara Ray has been involved in the training and trialing of border collies for more than twenty years. One of the top handlers in the country, Barbara is especially proud of her 2005 achievement of being the first handler in three years to complete the international shed in the Sturgis, South Dakota USBHCA/ABCA National Finals. In addition, Barbara has won some of the most prestigious trials in the United States over the years and has done consistently well in the USBHCA/ABCA Nursery program.

"I don't have the time to do severe corrections, and I don't like severe corrections anyway. I want a dog that is dying to please me."

How long have you been involved in sheepdog training and trialing? How did your involvement come about?

In 1979, I graduated from college and came home to the farm, where I expanded the family's flock of commercial sheep. Then I brought home a ram that carried footrot onto the farm; years went by trying to eradicate the problem. I had 400 sheep limping and crawling around on their knees. I was suicidal with depression over these suffering animals. I knew Don McCaig and his wife, Ann—Ann McCaig was my best friend—and they had just purchased their first border collie. Don told me where he bought their pup, so I went to the same person and bought a started dog, for which I paid a HUGE amount of money—$800! I brought it home, having had my half hour lesson, thinking all the while that this dog was somehow like Rin Tin Tin and would pick up with mental telepathy exactly what help Mom needed. The very next day I sent her into the woods to gather the flock, and she came back with only three sheep. Repeated efforts at the same task brought the same results. Needless to say, I was very disappointed. It became obvious that I needed some help with my new dog. Don McCaig was going up to Ethel Conrad's place for his second Jack Knox clinic, and I tagged along. That's where I learned that a trained dog is never actually finished: training is a process that continues throughout the life of the dog. So I learned all of my basics from a couple of years of going to Jack Knox clinics. And I had lots of fun; in fact, that was my social life, because otherwise I was on the farm trimming feet! I eventually had to stop attending these clinics because I kept coming home with new dogs. Jack believed that real experience was gained by training many dogs.

Did you study agriculture?

Yes. I had wanted to go to veterinary school. We didn't even have a vet school in Virginia, so the statistics were really out of favor for being able to do that—there were only four spots in Georgia and two in Ohio. I was not the brightest star in the state, so I wasn't able to get one of those spots. I received a degree in biology, with a strong emphasis in animal science, from Virginia Tech.

So your family farm always had livestock?

Oh, yes. We had cattle and a small flock of sheep, thirty head. I expanded the operation. I preferred livestock that I could actually flip over and handle. But the dog—her name was Panda, and I used her on cattle as well as sheep—was a great dog to start with: she had a lot of eye, and she didn't get into trouble. She wasn't the sort of dog that was nailing the sheep and riding them across the universe. So I think she was a good first dog. She was more the type that would come to the sheep and stop and stare at them, which for a novice person is a heck of a lot better than one that is going to be busting through the middle and grabbing them and flipping them over. Otherwise I would have thought that border collies were the worst things in the world.

So fast forwarding to the present, how many dogs do you start a year on average?

Well, I do a lot less of it now than when I was at the peak. I still train for other people, though. Now, I'm probably doing about 15 a year.

Are they all for clients, or are some for your own use?

Oh, no. About five are for me.

What do you consider the ideal age for starting a dog?

I'd say a year old. I know that that is later than most people start, but I have so much going on that if I start them beforehand, I have a lot of dogs getting into trouble. I can't allow them the freedom to run around outside the kennel or outside the house, because they are usually slipping over the hill and getting into trouble with the stock. So I do it on purpose. I know that at a year of age they are mature enough to be able to take my putting pressure on them. You know, I'd love it if I just had a simple life where I would sit around on the couch and eat chocolates, and go out and work my dogs whenever I wanted to. But it just isn't that way. I'm putting out fires in so many different directions that being able to work a dog is a luxury that I hardly ever get. So I want to make the most of it. There is no way I'm going to take my dog and introduce it to sheep at five months of age, because I know that once I do that if I have to stick the dog out the door and answer the phone, and maybe I'm on the phone for an hour, that dog will probably slip down to the sheep and start doing stuff that I would never have wanted it to do.

What age, if any, would you consider too old to get started? Is there a point that you think they've just missed the window of opportunity?

Definitely. I think it's an individual thing, though; each dog has its own window of opportunity. And, also, it depends on how it was raised. I just recently got one in, a two-year-old dog that was allowed to wander out in the fields with the farm's cattle. When dad drove up, it would run out and start messing with the cows. This dog has also never had pressure put on him, so he can't take a stranger asking him to respond to things that he's always had the freedom to refuse. Now, I don't think that it's because he's a two-year-old that it isn't working out; I think it is more because he didn't learn to take any kind of pressure in that time and he didn't really learn good from bad because he was not accountable.

What do you look for when you choose a puppy? What do you consider the ideal pup?

I like a friendly pup. I like a pup that is eager to engage with me. I usually judge a puppy among other dogs, and if it is much more interested in the other dogs than in me, I don't find it nearly as appealing. I like a pup that will respond to my voice: when I'm being really sweet, it will get excited about hearing the pleasure in my voice, and it'll be responsive when I change to a gruff note if it is doing something wrong. I like one that takes correction well.

How much do you look at pedigree in selecting a pup?

It is not pedigree so much as what the parents are doing. Sometimes if I have access to the pup of the International Supreme Champion, I might be interested in that. But if it is a pup off a dog that I've always admired, that is what I would go for.

Do you tend to prefer dogs or bitches?

I like bitches only because if they don't work out they are easier to sell. I think I get along with bitches better, but I find them less reliable through the year due to their cycle. They definitely change in the amount of pressure you can put on them and how reliable they are, according to their estrus cycle.

When do you like to see pups show an interest in sheep?

I think I like it as early as possible, because then I know I've got something to work with. I'm worried if it is not showing an interest by, say, eight months of age.

How old are your pups when you generally first introduce them to sheep—not start formal training necessarily, but expose them?

I'll take them to sheep even at four months old. I'll let them run about while I'm working an older dog and see what they do. I won't work in a tight space where they might get bowled over. Usually they are running around behind the other dogs, but some of them, of course, just boom right in there. When that happens, I take them away and I don't put them back with the sheep until I know that I want to start working with them. Again, that is mostly because of my lifestyle and because I have so very little time to deal with it. I guess so many people are able to do all the right things and put just the right amount of pressure—start them on ducks and that kind of stuff—and it is not by choice that I don't do that, it's just because I have so very little time. So I think the dog that works out for me has to be the type of dog that is really going to shine, and if it were being *neglected* it would shine anyway. That's why I look for all these special puppies with those personalities that are eager to please. Because if they are not connected to me, then it is not going to work out. I don't have the time to do severe corrections, and I don't like severe corrections anyway. I want a dog that is dying to please me.

How are your puppies raised?

I bring all of my puppies into the house on an individual basis in the evenings, and then I'll put them in a crate at night if they are in the chewy kind of phase. If they are real little puppies, I might even have them sleep in bed with me. But I really try to bring them into the house in the evenings so we can form a solid bond and start manners training. I have a four-wheeler, and I'll haul them around while I'm doing chores and stuff, so they learn to ride in a vehicle and to stay with me. I try to do it as young as possible, so they are used to feeling safe around me in uncertain environments. And when I do expose them to sheep, I drive them *way* away from the house—fortunately, I've got a big enough place for that—and I'll expose them to sheep in some back field that they'd never be able to find again.

What sort of sheep do you like to start a puppy on, and what size group?

Well, I usually start with lambs because they are smaller. I'll run them around a little bit with an older dog first so that they're not sticking their heads through a fence. I'll start out in a half-acre pen that I've got. And I'll usually have my young dog on a long line because it has become more difficult for me to catch him at the critical time. If they are really upset by the long line, then I have to take it off. I also have a rattle paddle on standby, because a young, eager dog might go in and latch onto something. It is a tricky time where you have to come up with a method that will encourage them to let go and to stay back but not discourage them from working at all. I'll try voice tone, I'll try the rattle paddle, I may use a bag, or sometimes it takes getting hold of the dog and shaking it. I keep changing methods until I find one that works for that dog, to get them so that they won't get in there and nail a sheep unless asked.

What do you think is the proper-sized group for introducing a pup to sheep?

Ten.

What do you like to see in a pup's first few sessions? What would tell you that the pup might be a good prospect? What might warn you of later problems?

Of course I would love to see a pup just leave my feet, go cast out around the sheep, and bring them to me ever so softly. That has never happened, but I can still dream! I like to see one that is obviously keyed in, one that shows some style about it—tail down, head down, and showing balance—interest in moving in response to my movement. Most of them don't show that balance, mostly in the first couple of sessions you have to manufacture that, and then hope that it feels good enough for the dog to maintain the sense of balance. Also, I like a dog to stay off of the stock: I just don't like a mouthy dog, a grippy dog that doesn't show improvement after a number of well-timed corrections.

Other than gripping, is there anything that you would just see and just say, "I'm not going through this again"?

Well, barking isn't very impressive, but I put up with it. A lot of times, a young dog will bark at sheep and then quiet down after the third or fourth session. I think a barky dog is thinking and trying to figure out how they can get the stock to move; they just haven't figured out the power of their eye yet. Barky youngsters usually figure out that they don't need to bark within the first few sessions; if not, I'd have it on the for-sale list. But if the dog will be used for cattle work, I can put up with it.

How about the sort that seem very afraid and don't want to engage with the sheep?

Well, yeah, a dog that is always quitting. That is probably the biggest reason that I have to make the phone call, "It is no longer economically feasible for me to have your dog." Which I try to do early on; I don't want to take a dog for three months and then have to give that speech.

What was the pup that you trained that showed the most early promise, and did it fulfill that promise?'

There have been so many, I can't say how many I've had, that have started out well and just didn't finish up well. I think that is one of the reasons that I start pups later now. Unfortunately, if it is starting really well and I've put a lot of time into it, I think I tend to put too much pressure on too early and the dog isn't mature enough to take that. So my method that has evolved is starting later, and working less. I put a tremendous amount of pressure on my own dogs in every work session; therefore, I don't take them out every day. I do other things, like taking them for long runs and swims and stuff like that, so they enjoy being around me and pleasing me, and then they're able to stand a long session (30 to 45 minutes) and the amount of pressure that I put on them.

Do you find that there is a correlation between the dogs that come along the most easily and the dogs that are the best in the end, or not necessarily?

I find it doesn't necessarily happen. What I've started doing with some of my pups is just sending them away from me for awhile, so that I'm not tempted to put too much pressure on them if they are going through a phase. My daughter is in college now, so she'll take a dog away and just expose it to a bunch of stuff that would never happen around here—huge numbers of people and activities. So the pup just learns to get out in the world and deal with all kinds of situations. And then they come back here, and they just love the work so much, so they seem to become even more connected because I've got that thing that they love to do.

At what age or after what amount of time in training would you give up on a pup that just wasn't progressing satisfactorily?

I called it quits with a Queen pup. That pup started out really well. And then when I started trying actually to shape her natural (unacceptable) outrun, or stop her from nailing sheep at the top, that kind of stuff, she would leave and go sniff. At first I lightened up and kept her. She never seemed to warm out of it—I gave her time off, I sent her off elsewhere, I stopped working her. And every time I went back, it seemed to get worse. So at age two, I sold her: now she's a wonderful house pet on a large estate and is as happy as can be. If I wasn't able to compete with her, she'd have picked up on the fact that I was disappointed and it just never would have worked.

What, if anything, would you expect your pup to know before you introduce him to stock?

I teach a lie down. I teach, "That'll do, here." I teach them to walk on a lead without pulling. That's basically it. I don't do tug-of-war with them. I understand that a lot of people do that with their puppies—they teach them, "get it, get it, get it." I've never done that. I've never taught them to be aggressive. I guess I'm so tuned into the sheep because I am a shepherdess, and I can't stand a dog that goes in and rips up something. I just won't let it go on. I will get heavy-handed to stop a dog from grabbing sheep. I just won't carry on for long with a dog that requires tough corrections and doesn't improve quickly. Dogs like that are often raised by people who allow or even encourage the young dog to be aggressive.

What is the progression of phases in your training program?

I take the pup into a small lot. I usually have an older dog that'll keep the sheep in the middle of the lot. I get it going around, doing the balance thing without attaching itself to anything. Then I do little walkabouts. Then I purposely put the sheep on the fence and teach the dog to get them off. Then I put them in a corner and teach the dog to get them out of it. Then I move away from the sheep on the fence, distancing myself some, and see if I can get the dog to go around, bring them off the fence and across the lot. If I can do all of that, then I take them out into a field. I'm very intent on teaching a dog outruns before I teach them to drive. I want them to outrun properly. Of course, I start small; I believe if they are not the right distance on a small outrun there is no point in getting farther away.

Is there a distance, a certain number of yards, that you want the outrun to be before you start the drive?

I'd say a hundred yards pretty consistently, and I like to see the first one *work*. I mean, you know how it is, you go out and the first time they latch onto something and you work out there, and you work out there, and you work out there, and you finally get a great outrun, and then the next day you go out and there you've got the same problem again. I don't move on if the first attempt isn't the right way. If I find the dog is taking too long to lift the sheep, then I start doing things like changing the number of sheep or the type of sheep. If the dog seems to have a problem coming on to something that doesn't move freely, I try to match the right kind of sheep with that dog to build its confidence. I can't help myself, when things are going well, I'm always going a little bit further than the dog is capable of doing just to always be challenging the dog. If the outrun did go well and the dog is bringing me the sheep, then I start trying to flank the dog. "Okay, you got that part, now let's try this." When I get out in the field, after I've got the outrun, I'll shorten up and actually start putting sides on the dog. I believe in putting sides plus a whistle on at the same time, right away. The stop whistle, the walk-up, the come-bye, and the way-to-me. The recall whistle is usually on my dogs way before I go to sheep. Then, when I've got that outrun at a hundred yards, I'll bring the sheep and start trying to drive. As I walk along, I usually always drive them back to the same place, then I'll call the dog off and outrun again. So they get used to it. "Oh, I know what we're doing, we're setting up for another outrun," the dog might think. And that seems to help them come to the driving faster. So it is not, you know, hours of walking beside the dog or walking behind the dog. I put the sheep to a particular place and set up the pattern so the dog learns to want to push the sheep to a place, then I call them off and they are so happy and you send them on the outrun and they are joyful because they get to bring them back. So it is not a really big, heavy change for them to get into driving.

How and when do you first introduce the stop on stock? Do you do that right there when they are first getting to balance in the small enclosure?

Yes, I do. I even try to get a little pace there. A lot of time it is completely different when you step out into the field. You've got everything under control beautifully in there in that little pen, and then you get into the field and it is like, "Wow, that dog shows a lot more push than it did in that pen."

When, if ever, do you start insisting on absolute obedience in your commands? How do you balance obedience with developing a pup's initiative?

I guess that is what makes me different from most, because I don't have absolute obedience probably on any of my dogs. I have always found that if I got absolute obedience in one area, it would probably be taking something from another area. For instance, I've got a dog that when I'm working a big group, like a hundred or so, she's always running around and clipping the heels. Clipping, clipping, clipping. You know, tucking, pushing, clipping. I generally have to gather up the hundred and then slice off ten or so to work, so it is constant. What goes through my mind when I see her clipping is the double lift, shoving twenty sheep around the course, and there she'll get a little heel and I'm done for, and I've just driven 2,500 miles for a DQ because I accepted this behavior at home. So I say, "Okay, I've got to address this issue," and I go in and I run at her when she does the clipping thing. She's not accustomed to my running at her, because she's always been allowed the freedom to work the sheep in the manner which she thinks appropriate, so after doing that I can end up with a dog who stands rather than takes action when something turns and looks at her for too long. She will un-doubtedly be thinking, "I can't touch these because, by gosh, Mom told me not to."

How do you handle pups who want to grip? Do you feel that gripping should always be addressed, or are there instances when you might ignore it lest you make the problem worse? What might your correction be?

I guess I'm of the belief that you have to nip it in the bud. I really think that if you don't, you are going to end up with dogs that grip. Of course, I want a dog to be able to grip when it is necessary to grip. After I teach them to stop gripping, then somewhere in their training I have to teach them to grip, that there is a time and a place for gripping—usually shoving them all into the barn or something.

Is that much later in their training? Are they pretty finished by that point?

Well, not finished but certainly when you are able to go out and do the farm chores with a young dog, it is time to teach it to grip.

So you teach a grip when the task requires a grip?

Yes. The methods for correcting the gripping depends on what kind of gripping it is. I try to catch the gripping before the grip happens. You can see there is a change in the young dog when it thinks about gripping before it actually grips. That is the important time to make the step to change the behavior. They change speed and they change angles before they go in and grip, and a lot of people start the correction after the dog has latched on and started riding the sheep across the lot. Yes, you need to do something there, too, but you should have started when the thought came into its mind. You say something, not necessarily yelling, but making note that you see what has come into its mind. I might throw a stick, or do something to make sure it changes its angle and its spot. I might grab their line, haul them in, and give them the full correction. If I don't have that, there is no way I'd go into a bigger field.

How early do you introduce shedding?

I really want the outrunning done, and maybe a little driving. I mean, I don't wait until the dog is two years old and just take up shedding when it is time to get into Open; I do it a lot earlier than that. But I want to make sure that the dog is balancing properly and under pretty good control. So it would be several months into the training before I'd start working on just calling the dog through the middle of the group and then taking part of the group away. It would be a *large* group though: it would *not* be where I had ten sheep and try to keep five away from five. Then I'll let the one group start back toward the first group from a big distance and try to get the dog to stop the ones running to rejoin the first group. So I guess it is not just shedding, it is being interested in facing the sheep that are trying to jump over the dog. And that is another culling point: if I can never seem to teach the dog to meet the challenge of the pressure from the sheep, it goes as a goose dog.

How about the look back? Do you like to introduce the look back with the shed, or do you like to keep them separate?

I introduce it with the shed.

When do you start to introduce whistles? Do you sometimes use different whistles for different sorts of dogs?

I introduce the whistles when I start the flanks, right in the beginning. I introduce all the whistles at once. I used to use different whistles for different dogs, but I don't anymore. I guess it is because I've run so many dogs with different whistles that when I'd trial I would end up using the wrong whistle at a critical time. So now I put all the dogs on the same set of whistles. But I have a wide variety of the way I give a whistle. So if a dog does need more, I can make any flank punchier and encourage a different type of performance out of the dog. I can do that—wide, fast, slow, that kind of thing —by changing the tone or the tempo of the whistle.

When you're building the outrun distance in the larger field, are you sending the dog from your feet initially, or are you moving to a point somewhere between the dog and the sheep in order to alter its path? What's your basic process for lengthening?

When I start out the outrun, I lie the dog down at an angle and reposition myself according to where the sheep happen to be. Once the short outrun is going well, I teach the dog to reposition around me. If the dog tends to run tight, I'll make sure to set it up wider from me before sending it off. I may even need to move closer to the sheep to prevent crossovers or extreme tightness. I'll run toward the sheep sometimes, which sometimes doesn't work—that sometimes just causes a competition effect that makes the dog want to see who can get to the sheep first. Sometimes I'll feel it necessary to put a stop on the dog on the outrun and intimidate it into taking a better angle toward the sheep before I'll allow it to go. Soon I end up with a dog who bends rather than stops every time I give it a stop on the outrun. At that point I'll have to go and reinforce the stop in other areas of our work, because I've probably taught it to widen every time it hears the stop and sometimes that is not what you want. Sometimes you actually want a stop! And that's yet another example of how fixing one thing can end up breaking something else.

At what point do you like to start entering your young dog in trials? What do you like to get out of these early trials? How do you go about choosing the best trials for your dog's development?

I probably put them in trials *way* too early. But then I don't go to that many trials anymore, and I think that trials are part of the training process. So when I enter a young dog in a trial, the last thing I'm thinking about is how competitive it is actually going to be. The trial is really more of a training session. I do, however, work on having somebody hold sheep for the dog before I go to the trial. I don't want that silly little factor to be the hold up in my being able to have a run or a learning experience for the dog. So I usually try to get that whole issue taken care of before I get to the trial. I just really want to know how the dog responds to me when I am putting pressure on it in public. Because I am a different person when I go to a dog trial, and my dogs look at me sometimes and go, "Who the heck is that?" My voice sounds different, and I just become competitive. And they are thinking, "Whoa, she was so sweet and easy at home. Who is *this*?" So some of them will seize up and others will get tighter and faster, and they just need to get used to my being different.

So you bring your young dogs to whatever trial you happen to be entering with your Open dogs, whatever the sheep and the conditions?

Yes, as long as I feel that they are not going to grab something in a situation where I can't call them off. If I felt like I had a good chance of them getting out around their sheep without causing harm, then I would go ahead and put them in a trial. For a novice person reading this and thinking that they should go ahead and do the same thing, let me add this comment: Don't! There is a big difference between a professional person and a novice person in that situation. The sort of poor timing of most novice handlers in their early days only serves to reinforce the idea that chaotic behavior is not only allowed but is actually encouraged.

Do you think that sometimes a dog learns something from retiring at a certain point, say when the dog keeps refusing a particular flank? Would you go ahead and retire to make your point?

No, I don't ever do that. I don't think that putting a dog away is a good correction. No, I don't believe in that at all. In fact, if I were going to retire, I'd go up the field and make that dog cast off and take that flank. You can't do that at every trial, so I would at least bring the sheep close enough to ensure an exaggerated flank before I retired. And then if I'm exhausting with my disobedient dog, I use that as a quiet training opportunity. Every time I exhaust with a dog I'm working on some part of something that disappointed me during the run.

Do you teach a stop at the top specifically, or do you prefer to train the dog to turn in on its own naturally? Or does it depend on the particular dog you're working?

It depends on the dog. If I had a dog that liked to come in hard at the top and run the sheep at me, and I didn't feel like it was making adjustments when I asked for them, then I'd teach that dog to stop at the top. Some dogs turn in short and blast in and move the sheep off sideways; I would teach dogs like that to back off, and I would encourage them to carry on a little beyond balance. When the dog turns in and moves back to balance, then I would ask for a stop. If I have a dog that has a hard time lifting, then I never put a stop at the top.

How do you feel about the USBCHA Nursery program? Do you generally like to run your young dogs in the Nursery class?

I love it. I absolutely love it; I just think it is great! It's like legalized gambling.

So you don't think it makes people push their young dogs along too quickly?

Oh, I think it does. I think it makes some people do that. And perhaps they are only interested in the competition and not the welfare of the dog. It is an individual thing. You are going to have all different kinds of things happening. I would probably run a dog that was way too young for the Nursery Finals if I felt it was a great training opportunity and I was going anyway. But I wouldn't take a dog that I thought was not ready—one that might embarrass me because it couldn't bring me the sheep, or that was going to latch onto something and ride it down the field. If I hadn't taken care of that part long before I went to the Nursery Finals, I certainly wouldn't be doing my job.

What's the most important tip that you would like to pass on to others who are interested in training a puppy?

I think that you've really got to love the dog. I have been more successful with the dogs with whom I have a good bond. Even though other dogs have been more talented, the ones that actually were connected to me, dying to please me—I guess that were considered more biddable—were the ones with whom I have been most successful trialing. Remember always that it's a partnership.

Derek Scrimgeour

KESWICK, ENGLAND

An eight-time member of the English National team and two-time finalist in the International Supreme Finals competition, Derek Scrimgeour has trained working border collies for many years. In addition, Derek's well-regarded training books and videos, as well as his popular training clinics, have helped him gain a reputation as a gifted communicator of his training methods to others.

"If you make a judgment too early, you can end up being very unfair as a trainer: you might think that your pup is one thing, and it's really something else entirely. I want to keep a really open mind."

How long have you been involved in sheepdog training?

I've been involved for over thirty years now. I basically started training dogs for work on the farm, and it became a hobby. I started out with a mixed farm that took in sheep for the winter. Back then, I had a limited number of sheep to train on and nobody to help me. So I actually tried to get people to train my first puppy, but no shepherd would take it on. So I ended up buying a trained dog from Tim Longton.

What made you decide that you wanted a dog at all?

I'd seen people working dogs on farms, but I'd never even been to a trial. Even when I went to my first trials, I didn't realize that you need straight lines in between the gates—I thought if you just hit the gates, you got the points.

How did you first get interested in trials?

My first introduction to sheepdogs was when I was about seven years old. I got bitten by one, and then I became very scared of dogs, so scared that it almost became a phobia. So my mother said that they were going to have to get a dog for me, to help me get over it. So they bought me a sheepdog puppy, as a pet. But it was also a sheepdog to work on the farm, and I just got interested in its training. That first dog we got wasn't a good one—she was weak and had nearly every fault you could imagine. But I didn't know any better, so I kept training her.

Do you take in dogs for training for other people?

I used to do that, but I don't do it as much anymore. Sometimes you'll train a dog, and it's a nice dog, but you know that you'll be giving it back to someone who could never handle it, so it's kind of wasted. And I don't have a lot of time to put into training dogs for other people, because if you have a good dog, you want to be able to buy it for yourself—it's hard to give up a good dog. And some of the other ones were just not good enough; you'd put a lot of time into training them, and they never got any better. So all in all, it was something that I didn't really like to do.

How many dogs a year would you say you're training these days, on average?

I used to train a lot of dogs, but now I'm doing a lot more training courses, so I don't do as much actual training. I have trained a lot of dogs in my life, but now I only train about four or five good dogs a year. I'm mostly busy with clinics and trials and competitions. I also breed dogs—just good stuff, trying to breed the very best that I can, and I also act as an agent to help people who want to purchase a dog find one. So selling the pups, giving training courses, and acting as an agent is about as much involvement as I want. I spend the rest of my time on the farm, because I enjoy farming.

What do you look for when you're choosing a pup for yourself?

A well-bred one, absolutely. I don't care much what it looks like. I want something off of parents that I like, that have bred well and work well. But given a well-bred litter, I'd take any pup—I wouldn't worry about which one.

Do you prefer one sex over the other?

I think males are better, because they don't have the hormone cycle every six months. But having said that, I've done very well with females.

How do you raise your pups? Are they in the house?

No, they're in a kennel. I have a feeling that if some pups are given too much exercise when they're young, it doesn't do their joints any good. It's best to keep them reasonably well fed, with a reasonable amount of exercise, but too much of it isn't a good thing. I shy away from starting them on sheep too early, because I worry about what it might do to their joints.

So when do you consider the ideal time for starting a young dog?

Well, I can't usually help myself—I usually take them out at first when they're about four months old, just to show them sheep and see if they're interested, not to work them. I just want to study them. I might let them run after the sheep a little, but I don't work them. Then I take them out again at about six months, and I like to see them doing a little bit then. But having said that, some dogs take about a year before they start, so I like to keep an open mind.

Do you worry if a dog turns on later than that?

No, I don't. I'm doing it as a business, of course, so the sooner they start, the sooner you can get something done with them, and the better it is financially. But as far as being a good dog, it really doesn't matter. Some dogs start at a year and a half, and some start at six months. It doesn't mean that the one that started at six months is going to be any better than the one that started later. The ones that start older tend to progress faster, in my experience. With the ones that start young, your expectations are so high that you expect them to be two years old when they're only a year old, because they started so early. I like them to start at about eight months, ideally— that's a good, sensible time.

Is there an age that you think is too old to start a dog?

I don't really know the answer to that one. I like to keep an open mind, but I'm sure that there *is* an age when it's much harder. Sometimes you can start a dog, but if you don't keep taking them out and getting them interested in sheep they can lose their initial interest. But I always see dogs at my clinics that are three or four years old and look promising, even if some of them haven't been trained very well. But I can see that if they *had* been trained to flank properly they'd be really special dogs.

What do you like your pups to know before you introduce them to sheep?

Very little in the way of obedience, because I don't want the pup to be focused on me too much early on. When I introduce the pup to sheep, I want him to be looking at the sheep.

Do you teach a lie down apart from the stock?

No, I don't really teach a lie down. I teach them to come to me with a "here, here," and I expect them to come in a very straight line right to my hand. I have a "that'll do" command, where I train them to come around behind me on the right-hand side if I slap my right thigh. If I want them to come round on my left, I slap my left thigh. I start them on that when they're quite young, and it ends up being something I use when I teach a dog to shed. It's really useful if you have it in place early on.

Do you let your new pup follow you around while you're doing chores, or do you like a more controlled environment for the first exposures to sheep?

I like a very controlled environment. I like quiet sheep that have been very well dogged, and I like to take them into the middle of a field. Then I like to let the puppy off and keep an older dog to hold them to me gently, just to make everything easy for the pup. At that point I don't want to do anything really except study what the pup is doing, just to see what's there before I start molding anything.

So you prefer a big field to a round pen?

Definitely. I've never got on well with round pens (or ropes, sticks, whips, or any of that). I don't find that I really need it. I use an older dog to help as long as I need to, but I find that after two or three lessons the older dog can go away.

Do you ever start a pup on livestock other than sheep?

No, I've never done that. I've always used sheep, quiet sheep.

How many quiet sheep do you like to use in your early sessions?

About six to ten. A bigger group can split, and then the pup can get in amongst them. It's harder to help the pup get control with a bigger group of sheep.

You've already mentioned that you don't like ropes, sticks, or whips. Are there any aids that you do like to use in your early training?

I use a short PVC rod (no more than about two and a half feet long) that I can slap against my leg to make a noise and reinforce my voice.

What do you like to see in a pup's first few sessions?

I like to see a pup show a lot of interest, and I like them to have the instinct to give a little room as it runs around sheep. And as it approaches the sheep, I like to see it dip its head a little bit, showing a little bit of style. And I like to see a desire to walk forward. But I try not to have any expectations; I want just to look and see what's there and not judge.

That's a difficult thing to do.

It *is* hard to do, but once you've made a lot of judgments you realize just how wrong you can be. If you make a judgment too early, you can end up being very unfair as a trainer: you might think that your pup is one thing, and it's really something else entirely. I want to keep a really open mind. For instance, a dog that seems at first to have no eye might develop eye later on, a dog that looks weak might develop more power, or a dog that looks like it's going to have a lot of power can actually end up weaker than you first thought when you train it up. Just try to keep an open mind and don't judge your dog. I sometimes go to clinics where people ask me what I think of their dog, and I say that it's too early even to *start* to think. I really don't like to judge a dog until it's trained; only then can you start to make some judgments. It does an injustice to the dog to make judgments before you can come close to seeing the finished article.

Even though you're trying to keep an open mind, is there anything that would tend to disappoint you about a pup's first few sessions?

There's really nothing that early that would disappoint me—I just don't think like that. I do like to see a sound temperament, something that's honest, wants to work, shows a little bit of effort in trying to do what you want, and tries to be helpful and responsive to you.

Can you think of a pup that you trained that showed tremendous early promise? And did that pup go on to become an outstanding adult?

The second dog I ever had was a dog called Laddie, and he was special right from the start. He was just an unregistered pup that I bought from a shepherd, and he was as good a dog as any I've ever had in my life. I was very lucky with him, and I learned a lot from him. He wasn't really easy to train—he was hard to check and he ran tight—but he had quite a lot of power and was very talented. He showed me what a dog is capable of.

Do you find that the dogs that come along the most easily are often the best dogs in the end?

Not at all—it's often the opposite. But not always, of course: some of the ones that start out well end up very good dogs in the end. But some of the ones that start out easily and look very, very promising just don't make it in the end. Some dogs that have a little bit more forward drive and upset sheep at the beginning are the best dogs ultimately. A dog that's a bit lighter and a good flanker always does well at Nursery trials, whereas a dog that's tighter in its flanks and a little bit pushy isn't going to win many prizes at Nursery trials, but that dog could become very good as an older dog. And some dogs that start out very flashy and flanky can get sour: they learn where pressure is, and sometimes they learn that it's not what they want. When the pups are younger they don't realize where the pressure is on the field. As they get older they start to realize where the pressure points are, and they actually try to avoid them. Whereas your stronger dog actually *wants* to be where the pressure is. So usually a stronger dogs ends up being the best one in the end.

How do you feel about the Nursery program in general?

I think as long as it's used wisely it's a very, very good thing— it's good for the people to get out there with their dogs. As long as you take your young dogs out, and you keep control of them, making sure that they'll drive properly and flank properly, and don't get carried away trying to win things. As long as you use Nursery trials as a training aid for your dog, they can be a great thing. It's hard to do that, especially if you win the first one—that makes you want to try to win the next one. But if you can avoid that temptation, Nursery trials can be very helpful in bringing your dog along.

When would you start to give up on a dog that you didn't think was progressing satisfactorily?

For myself, once I know that the puppy doesn't have anything "extra," any special talent, I'll just sell it quickly as a farm dog. As long as it's showing some special talent I'll train it right through and then maybe sell it as a trial dog or keep it for myself. But as soon as I know that it's only going to be a work dog, I'll just sell it on.

What would be the special kind of talent that you'd be looking for?

Just a little bit of special control; something that the dog does with its eyes. Little flanks that the dog shows me that it can do itself. A bit of an extra talent for controlling sheep that another dog doesn't have. Or a dog that can settle its sheep but still has the power to move them. I don't like gripping dogs at all. I don't mind a dog defending itself and turning back a sheep that's been aggressive, but I hate dogs gripping from behind—that's weakness, and it shows a bad temperament. I position myself when training pups to prevent that from happening, but if the pup persists in doing it, we'll part company. I don't want to breed that type of dog.

Can you give us a quick overview of your training progression?

I like the dog to be going around its sheep from the start. But instead of staying at that stage for a long time, the way a lot of people do, I like to move on to a driving situation, in which the dog is walking onto sheep: on a fetch, not driving them away, but walking them straight to you, and taking little flanks, not flying round and round. You have to get them going round and round at the start, but as soon as I get them doing that, I stop them to get them to walk up straight.

Are you getting them to do the little flanks on their own, or are you trying to command the dogs to do them?

They're little flanks that I'm trying to encourage. I'm not actually giving them the flanks—I'm just trying to position myself to make those flanks logical. I'm not making them do the flanks; I'm just putting words on while they're doing the flanks that come naturally to them because of my physical position. The dogs think that they're doing it on their own, but actually it's my position that's causing them to make that decision. I always want to put the dog in a position so that they think that they're making all the decisions. I don't, for instance, chase dogs around sheep; I move myself so that the dog wants to cover the sheep on its own. After the dog is comfortable bringing sheep to me and covering with little flanks I'll move myself from the fetch position, so that the dog is almost driving the sheep alongside of me in a little triangle. I'll be moving with the sheep, and as soon as I get the commands right and the dog is making nice shapes, I'll try to move myself out from the sheep and gradually wear myself behind the dog. I never have to call the dog in front of me to start driving—I like the dog to keep driving and I actually move behind it.

What about bigger flanks and outruns? When do they come into the picture?

Right at the start. I'm always trying to position myself in such a way that encourages a dog to make a nice shape.

So you're working on having the dog walking onto its sheep and the bigger flanks all at the same time?

Yes. I'm always trying to get nicely-shaped flanks without spoiling the dog's enthusiasm, or making them feel as if I'm forcing them to do it.

So if the sheep pass you when you're doing a fetch, would you ask the dog to flank and get them back?

Yes. I always want to let a young dog feel that he has control. And I'm also very careful about the voices that I use. For instance, I make sure that all of my "walk on" commands are said in a nice, inviting tone of voice. I also give both of the flanks—left and right—in an invitational voice. The only thing I use a strict voice for is the stop. So when the dog flanks, or walks on, it's always an invitation. You need to train your dog to love flanking, and love walking on—it has to be a really good experience, and if you shout at the dog, you'll make it a bad experience. The only thing that they get a loud voice for is the lie down, which has to be a demand, not an invitation.

So how do you go about introducing the stop, and when do you do that?

I just walk forward, and I try to block the ground before the dog gets there to stop it. You just jockey back and forth until the dog decides that it can't get past you and stops—at that point, you'll tell it to "lie down." Then just make the dog lie down for a second or two, and then put it into a flank. Don't try to hold the stop for too long. It's always done on the fetch at first, to make it easier.

What do you do with a dog who really fights with you about the stop?

I try to stop them less. I look for little windows of opportunity when the dog's mind is open to the possibility of stopping, and I make use of those. After a flank, for instance, there's a short moment where the dog is deciding whether or not to flank back the other way, and if you speak to it there and ask for the stop, it might be receptive. But if the dog has already decided to come back on that flank, it's too late; you've missed the opportunity. You've got to get to the dog in between these points of decision-making, to try to stop it there.

Do you insist that the dogs lie down on their bellies?

No—any sort of stop, even a hesitation, will do at first, and I'll try to build on that. And instead of going at the dog to make it stop, I'll go at the ground in front of the dog, making that ground a little bit dangerous. If I threaten the ground in front of the dog, the dog doesn't want to work on that ground, and it seems to work better for me.

When do you start teaching the idea of pace to your dogs?

Right from the start. As soon as the dog starts the fetch, I try to put a little "steady" on them; if I can't get a stop, a steady's enough. But I start to control the pace very quickly; I want the dog to know that when I say "walk on," it means walk, not trot. In my system of training, the initial approach to the sheep is always a walk, and if I want more, I'll ask for more.

How do you get that "more"? Do you worry that asking for pace too early will take some push out of the dog?

As the dog progresses, I always have in my mind that I want to be able to control the pace at all times. I'll take the dog out and do special training sessions on faster walk-ons—I'll clap my hands and encourage the dog to go faster, using sheep that move away. I want to make sure that the dog has at least two different speeds; with some dogs, you can get three speeds out of them. But two is good.

Do you use different whistles for the different speeds of walking up?

Yes. I use a slower whistle for a regular walk on, and a faster, more encouraging one when I want the dog to walk on a bit faster and actually push into the sheep. I have a third whistle that means really push into the sheep hard, even gripping them if it's the only way to move them. Sometimes I'll encourage a dog to grip and then stop it just short of gripping— that is, make it threaten to grip but not actually do it.

How do you go about lengthening and shaping the outrun?

I have a system where I stop the dog on its outrun if it's too tight. I walk up the field toward the sheep, past the dog, but not too threateningly. I kind of focus on a piece of ground to the side of the dog, and I warn the dog not to go into that ground. Then I ask the dog to flank again. When the dog avoids that piece of ground, it makes the shape that I want it to make. But of course, you've got to keep the dog's momentum going when you're working on the outrun—you can't stop the dog like that six times in a row, or it'll stop wanting to outrun. You might do it once in an outrun, then have another two outruns in which you don't do it, and then do it once again.

So you'll let the dog be tight sometimes?

If you have to. You never should kill the dog's momentum—if you kill the momentum, you've killed everything. So you'd want to work on the shape of the outrun over a period of months rather than of days. It wouldn't matter if it took a year, as long as it was right in the end. I like to take a long time to train—I don't want to rush things.

Do you spend a lot of time working on the top of the outrun?

I do that right from the start. As the pup starts to go around its sheep, I try to encourage it to go round properly and not be tight. And again, I try never to chase the pup—I threaten the ground to encourage the pup to avoid the spot that I'd like him to avoid. I want the pup to make the decision to avoid the ground that I'm threatening, so he can feel that he's in control of what happens. I don't force anything; I just tell the pup that this particular ground is really dangerous.

When do you start insisting that the dog really start obeying you perfectly?

With my way of training, obedience is something that just gradually creeps up. Each dog is different, but I find that if I keep asking for obedience without forcing it too much, it usually just comes naturally, just through repetition and practice. I don't like being too hard to enforce obedience, because I want the dog to *like* stopping, *like* flanking, and *like* walking on.

We've already talked a little about how you incorporate walking onto sheep from the very beginning of your training progression, but why don't you say a little more about how you develop and polish a drive in a young dog?

There are really two ways of teaching a drive. Some people like to get a dog flanking first, and then once they have a dog flanking and staying off sheep they try to get it to drive. But as soon as I see a drive developing, I go with the drive. I'd rather have the dog walking up onto the sheep properly on a fetch, get the walk right, and then put flanks onto a good walk, rather than put a walk onto good flanks. I want the dog to be able to walk up on the sheep balancing them properly from the beginning.

So you're teaching the dog to hold a line on its own?

Yes.

When do you introduce shedding?

Not until the dog is flanking properly and driving properly. Unless the dog's flanks are perfect, there's no reason to start shedding—it doesn't make sense to call the dog in among sheep one minute and then pushing it away from sheep the next. So I make sure that all of the flanks are really nice before I start shedding.

How do you go about introducing the shed?

I have about seven different steps for that—I take a long time to teach the shed. The first thing is to bring the dog straight through a group of sheep: the dog needs to come absolutely straight through, and right to me. If I don't get that stage, then I don't go on to the rest. If the dog wobbles at all as it comes in, it's going to be putting pressure on the sheep and making them want to group together again, so it needs to come absolutely straight. It's not difficult for pups that have been trained to come directly to a person's hand, but it's very important. I sometimes have problems when I buy dogs who haven't been trained to shed properly, and who have been allowed to come in by blasting into the middle any way that they like—it can take a long time to train dogs like that to keep their heads and to come in straight.

When do you start to introduce whistles?

Whenever I feel that things are calm enough with a pup, I'll add in the whistles.

Do you start with a stop whistle, or flank whistles, or doesn't that matter to you?

It doesn't really matter. I just do it when it feels right, when everything is nicely settled—then I can give the flank and the whistle at the same time.

When do you like to start entering your young dogs in trials?

Only when I know that they can complete the course, be obedient, and keep control of the sheep. There's just no point at all in running a dog in trials before it's ready, none whatsoever. If a dog isn't under complete control at home, it's madness to enter it in a trial.

What's the most important thing that you'd like to pass on to people training a dog?

That's the easiest question: when you're training a young dog and you find yourself getting angry, put the dog away—not when you *do* get angry, but when you *start* to get angry, just put the dog away and go have a cup of tea.

Patrick Shannahan

CALDWELL, IDAHO

Patrick Shannahan has been involved in sheepdog training and trialing for almost twenty years, winning the USBHCA/ ABCA National Finals in 1994 with his bitch Hannah. Patrick got his start in the livestock industry and has since developed his passion for training sheepdogs into a fulltime business, spending his days working with dogs, livestock, and people. His main goal is to provide practical dogs to help with the day-to-day management of working livestock ranches.

"I'm looking for a really good four- or five-year-old Open dog; I'm not really looking for a good two-year-old Nursery dog."

How did you get your start in sheepdog training?

I have been involved for about seventeen or eighteen years. It came about because I actually started with sheep about twenty years before I had my first dog. I had sheep, and I went over to a famous purebred sheep producer in Oregon, saw his dog work, and decided I was going to have one of those one day. So I got involved at first just to get a good work dog.

How long before you set your sights on trialing?

Well, I bought a puppy and then about six months later I bought a trained dog. At the time I didn't really think I'd be interested in trialing—I was actually showing purebred sheep—but I figured that if there was a trial that was convenient, I'd go. So, of course, I did: I did really well, I had a lot of fun, and that was the start.

If you had show sheep, I imagine they were accustomed to a lot of handling and such. Did that create a problem for training dogs? Did you have to start a work flock of sheep for the purpose?

No, I didn't. I had about 250 ewes. I just started working some of the lambs and let it go from there.

How many dogs do you start a year on average?

I start probably just two.

Do you start client dogs at all?

No, I don't. I used to do some custom training here, but I've been doing quite a few seminars, and it doesn't work well to be gone and try to train somebody's dog.

What do you consider the ideal age for starting a dog?

It really depends on so many different things. I don't know if there is an ideal age. I guess the ideal age is when you have time and when the dog is physically and mentally mature enough to do it. When I can commit a certain amount of time to training a young dog, that is when I would start it.

What age, if any, would you consider too old to get started if a client brought you an older dog for lessons?

I would tell them that you can always teach them things, but that there is a point of diminishing returns. You know, it takes a couple of years to get it trained. Usually a dog's best years are between four and seven, so you are not going to get the most out of it if it is starting the process as an older dog.

What do you look for in a puppy? What do you consider the ideal pup?

The parents. That's really all that I look at.

Are you looking at parents whose work you appreciate, or are you looking at a pedigree?

Yes, exactly, parents whose work I appreciate. Pedigree somewhat, but really more the work that I appreciate.

Do you think a pedigree gives you a sense of what sort of dog you can expect from a litter?

Not always. I feel like sometimes that really depends on the puppy. I think sometimes looking at the physical attributes of a dog you have somewhat of an expectation of what they are going to work like, how it is going to work for you. Since the parents have such a big influence, I mainly look at the parents.

Do you have a preference for dogs or bitches?

No, I don't. I like talented dogs of either sex.

How are your puppies raised?

The puppies that I raise I keep in the house until they are about four weeks old, and then they go outside. Then the puppy that I keep will come back inside. But I try to acclimate the pups to outdoor living before they proceed to their new homes, just because not everybody's puppy is going to live inside.

When do you like to see pups show an interest in sheep?

I'm not in as big a hurry as a lot of people. For instance, I have a six-month-old that I haven't taken out yet, but I'll probably start taking her out here pretty soon. But I don't have any doubt that she'll be keen. I haven't really had a lot of success, to be quite honest, with six- or seven-week-old puppies that are quite keen to work. Those for some reason seem to turn out to have lot more eye than I prefer.

How do you like to introduce the pups to stock—do you let them follow along while doing chores, or do you prefer a more controlled environment?

I control it. I'll take a nice group of sheep out and have a couple of older dogs with me to help out a little bit so that it doesn't get too wild and too out-of-hand. I don't like them discovering it on their own because they might decide that it would be fun to try to do that on their own when I'm not present.

So you wouldn't find having the older dogs there confusing for the young dog, or confusing for the older dogs?

I actually have dogs here that help me all the time with my lessons and with starting young dogs, so it's not confusing for them at all. I don't use my trial dogs for that sort of thing.

How old are they when you start formal training?

Whenever they are mentally ready to handle it, to respond to pressure and corrections.

Is there anything in their behavior off sheep that gives you an indication that they are ready to handle it?

I probably look for it more on sheep, to be quite honest.

So you'd take them to sheep, and if they didn't seem ready you'd put them up for a time?

If I were giving them a correction for a certain behavior and they couldn't seem to make the connection between the correction and the behavior, I'd assume that they were not old enough.

What sort sheep do you like to start a pup on? How many sheep do you like to use?

I have a flock of Katahdins, so I usually start them on that. I'd use seven or eight or ten, or whatever comes out. I'd start with a few more than I would normally have out.

Do you ever start on something other than sheep, say ducks or goats?

No.

What size field do you prefer for starting a pup? Do you ever make use of a round pen?

For my own dogs, I use a forty-acre pasture with the older dogs. At a clinic I may set things up differently. I usually use a round pen in that case for a couple of reasons. Number one, I don't have control over the stock the way I would at my own place. Also, we don't always have the same time that it might take to be out in an open field. A round pen is a great tool, as long as you understand that it is just a tool and you work toward getting them out of there as they gain experience.

Are there any aids that you make use of as a general rule, say a whip or a pvc pole?

I use different tools at different periods. But a tool is just a way to help you get a message across, and then you need to wean yourself off of the tool. So I wouldn't say that I have a certain tool that I use at a certain age or anything like that. Every individual is different. I try not to use any tool if I don't have to.

Would you take them out on a light line initially?

No, I try not to take them on a line at all, to be quite honest. I try to have them respecting me when we walk out, so even if the sheep are there and the dogs are kind of anxious to go they stay with me until I tell them it is okay to leave. If not, we try to work on that, but for the most part I have success.

What do you like to see in a pup's first few sessions? What would tell you that the pup might be a good prospect? What might warn you of later problems?

Ideally, I'll have something that goes around and balances fairly nicely and actually can feel the point of balance. Some dogs have to have that developed a little bit. When I'm looking at a young dog, I like to see them have nice flanks, and nice feeling or nice pace on the sheep. Those are two things that I look for. The other thing that I look for is a dog that is aware of me and wants to become a team. What I don't like to see are pups that are totally out there for themselves, and if they haven't gotten their way they shut down or decide that they prefer not to work. Those are the difficult ones. The ones that are actually really soft as far as corrections, where they possibly might shut down, are the most difficult for people to train.

What was the pup that you trained that showed the most early promise? Did that dog end up being as promising as it started out? Are dogs that come along the most easily the ones that are the best in the end?

I think there are a couple of different ways to be successful at this. One is to have an extremely talented dog and be a good handler. Second is to have a nice dog that makes a great team partner. And they are not necessarily the same. I see lots of teams that do pretty well, but if I broke it down and really looked at the dog I probably wouldn't prefer its method, or the way that it handled the stock, but the handler and the dog have formed a nice team and got that all put together. Does that make sense?

In the latter case, do you mean the sort of dog who is absolutely obedient and goes wherever the handler puts it?

Exactly. Then the other possibility is the dog that has a lot of talent and the person is able to let that talent come through. I've had both kinds of dogs. You can see the ones that are quite talented early on. As long as they want to be team players, the dogs that have the most talent are usually the ones that are the easiest to bring along.

Does a specific dog come to mind?

Just lately I'd have to say Riggs. He came along really early. I didn't start him early, but I got him fairly young. He just always wanted to learn and always wanted to please.

At what age or after what amount of time in training would you give up on a pup that just wasn't progressing satisfactorily? How soon would you make that determination?

For the most part, I would hope that I would give it enough so that it could make a nice work dog, even if it wasn't going to be a trial prospect. That would be my first goal, to get a nice work dog out of it. If it makes it as a trial dog, that would be a nice bonus, but not all dogs can make a trial dog. Most of us aren't really looking for good dogs anymore; we're all looking for great dogs. So sometimes if I determine that it isn't going to be a great dog for me, if I have the opportunity to place it in a good place, I will.

As a farm dog?

As a farm dog, or it might make a really great trial dog for someone else. But if it's not going to make it for me, then I'll probably put it somewhere else. I can only keep so many dogs, and even if I could physically keep all of them, the more dogs I keep the less attention each one gets, and the less I actually enjoy it.

What would be your ideal scenario? How many Open dogs would you like to keep, how many Nursery dogs would you like to have coming along?

I would like to have a couple of Open dogs, a couple of Nursery-aged dogs and a couple of pups. I have three Open dogs now, but I usually only run two.

What, if anything, would you expect your pup to know before you introduce him to stock?

I would hope that it would have a recall and it would have respect for me. So if it started to do something that displeased me, I could communicate that, and it would react appropriately. It needs to know to come when called, it needs to know to get into its kennel, it needs to know not to jump on me, or if it is doing something wrong I can tell it "no" and stop what it is doing.

What is the progression of phases in your training program? What skill do you start with, what and when do you move on to a new skill?

The first step is learning balance and method, so that the puppy develops its method of how it is going to move stock. When a puppy first works stock, it moves stock through its physical being, but I would work on it so that it learned to use its eye and it could use its physical being if it needed to at times. Learn to stay off, learn how to pace, learn how to rate. Then the next step would be to introduce and start working on gathers. The next step I just introduce driving, and with driving comes longer gathers. And with longer gathers, the lie down, the right and left, and the whistles.

How and when do you first introduce the stop?

It's probably four or five months before I actually put a real good stop on my dogs. If I used it too early, I'd use it as a crutch and I wouldn't teach them to pace and to feel their stock. If I have it on them, I'll use it, so I prefer not to teach it to them until later on.

Do you require the dog to stop with an actual lie down on its belly, or do you prefer asking the dog to stop on its feet, or does it depend on the dog?

Yes, it depends on the dog. Some dogs prefer to stand, and as long as they are stopping, I don't usually care if they are lying down or not. For students training their first dog, I'll make them put a lie down just so they have that as something they can resort to. After they've trained a few dogs, then they can change.

Do you prefer to stop your dog at the top when trialing, or let the dog turn in on its own?

I usually have them turn in on balance on their own, but they will listen to me, hopefully, so that I can stop them short or force them to go a bit longer.

How do you go about lengthening and shaping the outrun?

Once I get the shape of the outrun done, I usually let it to develop. If the shape is correct even if the outrun is a little tight or something, I just wait for it to develop. If the parents are good outrunners, I know that I have time to train that part of it if I really need to, but I'd rather have it to develop on its own. I let the dog make mistakes and understand why it couldn't get the sheep or why the sheep ran off.

Would you stop them on the outrun if it was too tight as a rule, or wait and see if that becomes a chronic problem?

No, I probably wouldn't stop them but I'd probably go correct them. Because there they are not really using their method.

When, if ever, do you start insisting on absolute obedience in your commands? How do you balance obedience with developing a pup's initiative and confidence?

I think that when they are young, they have to adhere to it more than when they get older. I'll trust them once they have the experience. But everybody is a different individual. For instance, I have dogs that know how to hit a panel, so if I'm not careful and I don't use their judgment and I insist on obedience I'm going to miss it. So I prefer that they handle it on their own.

How do you handle pups who want to grip?

I think what most people don't really understand, and this is where they get it wrong, is that they get mad at the dog for gripping, but gripping is really just a result of the action that is wrong in the sense that they are too tight. So the proper correction would be to correct them for being too tight, not for gripping. Eventually, most of us are going to want to have a grip on our dogs, or a bite command, and we don't want to take that out. I want the dog to know that if needed, they can always bite.

Do you set up a situation and formally train that?

Yes, just depending on the individual. All of mine, I hope, know that if it were really necessary I would let them. They know the difference between what is a trial and what is work. I hope that they would know that as long as it is necessary, I would respect that.

So what would be your process, in a nutshell, to teach a dog to hit a nose properly? Do you teach that in a chute?

Most of the time it would just be out in the open and I would just grab a sheep and get the dog excited with my voice.

If you have a pup that seems only to want to drive or only to gather, does that influence when you teach the outrun or when you introduce the drive?

I don't know, occasionally there has been a dog that has kind of gone out of sequence just because they couldn't get the gather and I had no other way to teach them anything, so I started teaching them to drive first and then went back to the gather. Sometimes, you know, it is important to wait until you have enough tools so that you can fix a problem, enough tools on the dog so that you can fix something that is not right. If you have a puppy that doesn't know much and doesn't have much experience, you don't have many tools to help it. So you have to wait to fix it until you have the tools to teach it properly.

How early do you introduce shedding?

I guess lately I've been just doing it earlier and earlier. If I see opportunities for a pup that is even a year old, I start calling him through. I don't make a big deal out of it, but I want him to know that occasionally it is okay.

So initially it's just a recall through two groups?

Yes, if there is a big gap between the two groups of sheep, I just call him through to me.

Do you like to introduce the look back with the shed, or do you like to keep them separate?

I like to keep them separate. I don't want the dog always to assume that when there is a shed they are just going to go back and get the other group of sheep right away.

Do you sometimes use different whistles for different sorts of dogs, or are all of your dogs on the same set of whistles?

That is what I do now. I've done it where each dog was on a separate set, but currently they are all on the same set. I have really no need for a brace at this point. I modify the whistles for each dog, so if I have a dog that needs more excitement or more calming I can slow it down or speed it up. But they are all on basically the same set of whistles.

At what point do you like to start entering your young dog in trials? What do you like to get out of these early trials? How do you go about choosing the best trials for your dog's development?

As long as the dogs are learning from the situation and learning positively from the situation, I'll enter them. Of course, I have to wait until they can do a Pro-Novice or Nursery type course. Even if the sheep are difficult, if the dog is listening well and working well I'll continue on. If the situation is over the dog's head and there is not going to be much value in being out there, I'll either pull the dog or quit when I think the situation is not of any benefit.

Would you say that your dogs are usually well prepared for the class that they are entered in? If it is a two-hundred-yard outrun, would they be running out three hundred yards or more?

Most of the time they'd be overly prepared. Occasionally—that is what a trial is—it is a challenge. Hopefully, they've had that distance but they might not have been prepared for it on that type of sheep or circumstance or that type of terrain.

If you are going to be at a trial to run your Open dogs and the young dogs are coming anyway, might you enter a young dog in that situation perhaps a little before it is ready?

Yeah, I have one that is maybe not quite ready but she's been running well and listening well, and the trial might be a tiny bit over her head, but I don't think it has been any detriment to run her. Out here we might get an opportunity to run on range sheep, and that is just great experience as long as the dog is running and listening well.

Have you ever had experiences on the range sheep with young dogs where the dog got injured or scared off by an experience that required rebuilding the dog's confidence?

If I see something happen at a trial, I'm not afraid to leave the post and go out and help the dog. I've seen a few people that have damaged their dogs for some reason, maybe the competition or their ego, and tried to make a situation work that wasn't going to work. If the dog is not learning from the situation and it may be causing harm, it is my job to get out there and help it get out of that situation.

What is your feeling about the USBCHA Nursery program? Do you generally run your young dogs in the Nursery class?

I participate sometimes if I have dogs that are ready. I personally wish they'd change the dates a bit. I think that it is a tiny bit unfair for dogs that are born in May or June to have to compete with dogs that are almost a full year older. But I think it has been really good for the USBCHA and border collies in general. I think it helps bring dogs along.

Would a pup with a desirable birth date interest you more than one with an unfortunate birth date, say a May or June pup? Would that factor into your decision to get a pup or not?

No it wouldn't, to be quite honest. If I wanted a pup I would get the pup. It is like Nursery, if it conveniently works out I'll do it, if it doesn't, that's fine as well. I'm looking for a really good four- or five-year-old Open dog; I'm not really looking for a good two-year-old Nursery dog.

Do you think the attributes tend to be different, or do you think there is a good deal of overlap?

They can overlap. It's not that I wouldn't keep a dog that couldn't be trained really well until it was three, but I probably wouldn't want it in my breeding program. Just because I don't want to have to wait until they are three to see if I'm going to like them or not. But just because my dog doesn't make it into the Nursery program doesn't mean I'm going to get rid of it. Most of them I don't get rid of.

What's the most important tip that you would like to pass on to others who are interested in training a puppy?

I would say find a mentor that you respect because of how they work with their dogs and their relationship with their dog, and if they can't give you lessons or be your trainer, have them suggest someone that could work with you in a similar style. Don't get too much advice from too many different people.

Jeanne Weaver

WILLIAMSTON, MICHIGAN

Jeanne Weaver has been training and trialing border collies since 1996. In recent years, she and her bitch Liz have had much success in some of the most prestigious trials around the country. Liz (who won the Canadian National Finals in 2006) has qualified for the USBCHA/ABCA Finals every year she has run in Open, regularly advancing beyond the first round of that competition. Liz has also qualified for the double lift of the Bluegrass for five straight years and continues to be a strong trialing partner for Jeanne.

"Practical work is very important in bringing a young dog along. The dog is going to learn to trust you if you understand and can read livestock and you allow that dog to keep the stock under control."

How long have you been involved in sheepdog training and trialing?

I had Australian shepherds for many years (I think I started with Aussies in 1976), and I ran them on sheep and cattle in the arena trials. I got involved with border collies in the mid-1990s—I think I got my first one in 1994, from Marilyn Fischer. I started competing in 1996.

Was that with a dog you trained yourself, that you bought as a puppy?

Yes. And by then I also had Don, who had been given to me by Red Oliver. Red came up to visit, and he had a whole litter that he had shipped out to 4-H kids to be raised, who were at that time about eleven months old. He asked me if I wanted one of them. I said sure, and that dog became my Don. And I also bought Henna, from a woman in California, and she was a daughter of Glyn Jones's Lad that he had imported to Virginia. So I was running Hail in Pro-Novice, and Don and Henna in Pro-Novice and Nursery that year. I didn't feel that it was right for me to start in Novice, because I had been competing with the Aussies for so many years. Both of those dogs qualified for the Nursery Finals that year, and I ran both of them at the Finals in Lexington.

When you start dogs now, are they mostly client dogs, or are they dogs that you're starting for your own purposes?

Probably more client dogs, although I don't take a lot of those; I don't take more than four at a time. For one thing, I don't have the room, and for another, I want to be able to spend some time with my own dogs. But I probably don't start more than one or so a year for myself, and not more than eight or ten for other people.

Is that one dog a year that you start for yourself usually something from your own breeding?

Yes, usually.

What do you look for when you're choosing a puppy from litters that you've bred?

I've come to the conclusion over the years that the best thing to do is to take the one that's left. They change a lot as they grow and experience the world—the most outgoing pup as a little one might not end up that way as an adult. Even if they grow up next to each other, things can change: the keenest, boldest one as a baby puppy might end up totally different.

Do you have a physical type that you prefer?

Not really; I don't care if they're smooth, or hairy, or anything like that. I do, of course, care that they're mentally and physically sound.

Do you prefer males or females?

Well, I get along better with males, but Liz has been a really good dog for me. Still, I do have to say that I like the males better.

How do you raise your pups? Are they in the house?

It depends on the time of year, but I usually start them in the house until they're old enough to go out. If it's cold, they need to go to the kennel when they're six or seven weeks old. If it's a warm time of year, I have a pen in the back yard that I can keep them in, and then I can spend some individual time with them. I don't think it's important that they get a *lot* of individual time, as long as they get *some* time. But the pup that I end up keeping will live in the house, and I like to keep him there until he's old enough to start. At that point, he'll usually go off to the kennel.

What do you like to work on with your pups before they go to sheep?

I'm pretty bad about putting a lot of obedience on puppies. They learn to be responsible for themselves, but a lot of my pups never even get leash trained. But they learn to come when they're called, to hang out with me, to move with the rest of the gang when we all go for walks.

So you don't teach a "lie down" off of stock?

No. I know that I should, but I really don't. But it seems to work out all right for me.

When do you like pups to show an interest in sheep?

The later the better! If they're very keen when they're little baby puppies, you'll need to be a lot more careful about where you let them tag along. If they start showing an interest at six or seven months, that's good.

Do you let the pups who haven't turned on yet follow you around while you're doing chores?

Yes. And we go for walks—the whole gang and I go for walks twice a day out in the pasture. So the pups learn to come along from the time that they're really little. I don't purposefully set things up so that the pups encounter stock before they're ready to work, but I have sheep all over the place; it would be impossible for them to walk around and not see the sheep. I certainly don't let them lie around and watch sheep, but they see sheep as they're growing up.

What do you consider the ideal age for starting a young dog?

That depends on the dog. I don't like to put any pressure on a dog until it's ten or eleven months old, but some dogs actually *need* that pressure and are ready at seven or eight months of age. But you're always taking a big chance of doing damage if you have a super-keen pup who needs pressure put on it at an early age.

How do you know when the pup finally is ready to take training pressure?

When it shows some common sense and acknowledges the fact that I'm actually in the picture. I've never really thought about that—it's just something that you get a feeling for. They need to show that I can be part of the picture pretty easily. The pups who aren't ready are the ones that you're basically invisible to; they're so keen and so focused on the stock that they don't see anything else. And a lot of young dogs will start out that way, regardless of how old they are. But if they're seven months old and they're doing that, I don't want to be putting a lot of pressure on them. All of a sudden they might conclude that they were punished for wanting to work, and it could really make a difference in their attitudes later on.

Do you think that there's an age where a dog is just too old to be started?

If it's in them, they can learn. I have a guy coming to me right now for lessons whose dog is eight years old. He brought the dog to another trainer who trains in a much different way, and the dog has a lot of faults. But you can tell that she's a good dog underneath, and he's going to be able to straighten her out. And mainly, he's going to learn a whole lot with her, even if she's retirement age by the time she's trained. And she's going to enjoy it. She's bred well enough that if she comes along in the next year he could run her in Novice or Pro-Novice, depending on how she ages.

Tell me how you introduce your pups to stock—do you do something formal?

I have a small 60 x 60 pen with the corners rounded off, and I just like to walk in there with the pup. And it depends on the dog—if the dog isn't showing much interest, I'll just walk along, move the sheep, and make exciting noises. If it still isn't showing any interest, I'll take it away and bring it back in a day or a week or a month, depending on the situation, until the dog starts showing interest. With my own puppies, I'll do this casually, just to see what's going on with them. With my student dogs, I'll go to a lot more trouble to get the pups turned on, because they've come a long way to have me work with them.

What do you mean by "go to a lot more trouble"?

Oh, running around, making funny noises, running the sheep off.

Do you think it ends up being better for the dog just to wait and let it happen, the way you do with your own pups?

I don't know that it ultimately matters. The big difference is that I'm not really in a rush to get my own pups started—if they're not ready, they're not ready.

What do you like to see in a pup's first few sessions? What would tell you that the pup might be a good prospect?

Well, my dogs are all so different, and they all started in such different ways, that it's really hard for me to generalize. What would excite me? I guess a really strong desire to keep everything together, to keep everything covered. I wouldn't care if they were a little wider, or a little tighter—even getting so tight that they start to cause problems—because a lot of times a looser-eyed dog will blast into the sheep and be really tight. I want the dog to move off of me a little bit, to show that he's aware that I'm there.

What type of sheep do you like to start pups on? And how many do you use?

It's really, really important to have dog-broke sheep—that's probably the most important thing of all in starting a pup. You absolutely don't want anything that's going to challenge the pup, or that's going to be uncontrollable. You want that pup to succeed. For the pup's first couple of sessions, I really want the sheep to be able to stay right with me, so the pup can succeed and I can be right there without the pup having to go berserk trying to control everything. After the first couple of times, I'll usually be able to get out of the small pen. Once I'm in the pasture, I might use those same sheep for another few sessions, gradually making things a little tougher.

How many sheep do you like to use?

In that pen I like to use three or four, because I don't like getting run over and getting my toes stepped on.

What breed of sheep do you prefer?

I have a mixture of hair and wool sheep in a flock of about twenty that I use just for starting young dogs and giving my lessons. Since I have such a mixture, I can make the sheep really heavy, really light, or anything in between. I can throw in, for instance, one anchor sheep who's pretty heavy, and a couple of lighter ones that will move off of the dog easily but who will stay with the anchor sheep if the dog is even halfway right.

Do you ever use any livestock other than sheep?

I don't. I had some goats for awhile, but they kept getting hung up in my feeders. I have a few cows around, but I just use sheep for starting pups.

Do you have any training aids that you like to use regularly?

I use things like a short stick or a longe whip with the short string around the end that makes a little popping noise, or often just my hat.

Do you use those aids from the very beginning?

It totally depends on the dog. Sometimes I never have to use anything. Sometimes I need it when the pup is so focused on the stock that I need to get their attention. And sometimes they're really keen and want to bite, and you don't want that happening, so you'd want to use something to put a little pressure in that particular spot.

So you correct gripping right away?

It depends on the dog and the situation. I try to be in the right place at the right time to keep it from happening. I want to build the dog's confidence up rather than tear it down. If they go in and bite once in awhile I'm not terribly concerned about it. But if I have a real aggressive dog who just likes to bite, I'll get after him. Even with this kind of dog, showing them that they can control the sheep without biting or trying to catch them will most often solve the problem. I think most dogs often bite because they're afraid or lack confidence.

How would you know that the dog was afraid rather than simply aggressive?

That's a hard one—it's just a feeling that you get about the dog in general. Some dogs just come into that ring with a "let me at 'em" attitude, and they might blast into the middle or cut one off and grip. They need some attention-getting exercises pretty quickly. But a dog who comes in and acts like it's a little worried about getting around the sheep, and maybe its tail isn't quite right, and grips when it has to go between the fence and the sheep, is telling me that it lacks confidence.

What about a pup who was gripping because it wasn't completely serious about the sheep?

That sort of pup probably isn't really ready for training yet. If they're not trying to control the stock, if they're just running around with their tail in the air, than they're not ready.

How long do you stay in the small pen with the pup, and where do you go after that?

With some dogs, it's only one session before we move out. With some dogs it's four or five times or even more, depending on the situation—rarely more than a week. But the length of time that they spend in the small pen doesn't necessarily correspond with how talented the dog is, or how well it's going to take to training. The dog who's in there for a week might be better than the dog who's been in there for two days. The dog who's in for only two days might be sensitive to the fence and be uncomfortable, so you'd want to get him into a bigger area pretty quickly. And I have another little area that's about 100 by 200, so that works well, and then I have a thirty-acre field. I really try to get them into the thirty-acre field within a few days.

What do you want them to master before they go out into that thirty-acre field?

Just control: controlling the sheep and being aware of me. With some dogs, I'll want them to have a good stop on balance. (I certainly wouldn't be expecting them to be stopping off balance yet).

What do you mean by "some dogs"? Why do you only want that on some and not others before you go to the big field?

Some dogs are softer and more sensitive than others. I don't want to be asking those dogs to lie down much—I want to keep them moving. Some dogs also have quite a bit of eye, and I want to keep those dogs on their feet and flanking. Every dog is so different that it's really hard to come up with any set of rules for all of them.

When you go to the big field, do you ever use an older dog to hold the stock in place?

Rarely. It's just too hard on my older dogs.

Tell me about a dog that you started that you thought showed great early promise. Did that dog continue to develop into an exceptional adult? Do you think in general that dogs who show early promise have the best chance of becoming the best sheepdogs?

Probably the dog I've had that was the easiest to start and train was Jack, whom I'm running now. I really enjoy him, and I think he's a great dog. But he's not the *only* great dog. He just was a little easier to start, a little more natural to start. He's a really good listener.

Did you have any dogs who were a struggle to start but who ended up being really excellent dogs in the end?

Liz was tough to start—very pushy and bossy, and I had to get in her face a lot. And she's made a great dog, but she's a very different sort of dog from Jack, much pushier. Jack's different; he's got more eye, and he's a lot more willing to play along, even though at the same time he's very natural.

What do you think are the easiest types of dogs to train, especially for novices?

I think a middle-of-the-road dog, without too much eye, but not too loose-eyed, with enough natural instinct to overcome a beginner's mistakes and all the handler errors that beginners have to go through while they're still learning. It should have enough confidence in itself, but not so much confidence that it wants to take charge of everything.

What sort of dog do you think would be really tough for a beginner?

A super-keen, super-fast, super-hot dog is a dog for experienced trainers. If you start putting that kind of dog in the wrong place all the time, and if they're not trusting you, they're just going to go out and do their own thing.

At what age, or after what amount of time, would you give up on a dog who just wasn't progressing satisfactorily?

I've learned over the years that sometimes it can take until a dog is two or three before you really know what you have. And they come along in different ways. I have a young two-year-old now that I didn't like at all for a long time, because he's very cautious when he learns new things—he's very slow until he really understands something. I thought that the dog was never going to have enough push for me. But as he's progressed, he's become quite pushy and responsive, things that

I never thought that I'd see in this dog. And all that started happening after he was twenty-two months old.

Can you tell me a little about the progression of training phases in your training program? What process do you follow when you're training a young dog?

Of course, it depends on the dog, but I think I basically do what most people do: I want the dog to cover, I want the dog to control its sheep, I want it to have a reasonably good stop on balance. After that, I just start gradually extending the outrun, gradually getting the stop a little better, depending on the dog. (If it has a lot of eye, I don't want to be stopping it a lot.) From there, depending again on the dog, sometimes I'll ask him to drive a few steps past me, and if they're getting comfortable with that I'll extend it out a little more.

Do you start driving before you teach the dog its flanks?

No, not really. If it's a looser-eyed dog, I'll do both at the same time. The thing is, they're always hearing the flanks, even if I'm not enforcing the flanks yet—if they're going come-bye, I'll tell them "come-bye." If a dog has more eye, I'd start working on flanks before teaching them to drive, and I'd also work harder on stretching the outrun. Some dogs are a little more natural driving dogs, and they can just fall right into it. A lot of times with training, if you see something that the dog really wants to do and is going to excel at, you just let it happen.

But wouldn't dogs with too much eye be the dogs who naturally want to drive? Would you let those sorts of dogs start driving?

A dog with too much eye (one that's sticky, who doesn't like to flank, whom you have a hard time moving) isn't a dog that I'd want to keep to train for myself, even though I'd train them for other people. A dog who truly has too much eye is not a dog that I'd want to start driving with early. But a dog that has a reasonable amount of eye while still remaining very flexible, a dog that uses his eye properly, is a dog that I can start driving with early.

How do you go about introducing driving?

I usually start driving by just letting the dog push the sheep past me for a few steps, and then turning around and going with them. Depending on the dog, I'll just gradually let them get farther away. The main thing is that I don't want to do any flanking until that dog is really comfortable pushing sheep and really understands the job: I want that dog just to take the sheep and go. It's really important that the dog always feel in control when they're learning to drive. If you're asking the dog to drive and the sheep are getting away from him, he's never going to want to stay back there; it's just not going to be comfortable for him. If the sheep start getting away, I'll stop the dog, flank him around, and have him bring the sheep back to start again. That way bringing back those sheep is my idea, not his; it's something that I'm telling him to do. I know that a lot of people wouldn't agree with doing it this way, but it works really well for my dogs.

How do you go about stretching the outrun?

That also depends on the dog. I don't like to put pressure on a dog unless I have to. So I usually just stand between the dog and the sheep and then send the dog. If the dog is showing a good feel for its sheep and covering well, then I'm going to gradually just start sending it five or ten feet farther. As long as the dog is thoughtful and covering, I don't care whether or not it's giving the sheep a lot of space. Then I'll just gradually move back farther and farther. If I start having problems, then I'll shorten it back up. I like to just draw the outrun out because it's usually there in the dog—only very rarely is it not.

What about fixing the top of an outrun?

If the top is flat, then I'll stand closer to the sheep. I don't want to put a lot of pressure on the dog, but if I have a serious problem with a dog who really wants to be tight and isn't learning to give its sheep room, then I'll start trying other methods. And usually there are several other methods that you can use, and I try the whole repertoire until I find out what works for that particular dog.

What are some of those methods?

A lot of the time it's just slowly walking down the field straight at the sheep as the dog is running out, which will tend to send the dog deeper. And then, of course, you take the pressure off as soon as the dog's right, by backing back up. The sheep can make things different, too. A lot of time if you're starting the dog out on heavy or very dogged sheep, the dogs *know* that they don't have to go deep to control those sheep. But if you put out lighter sheep, the light bulb goes on, and they figure out that they need to give them more space. I like to let them figure out those things on their own, but if that doesn't work I get serious about shaping it.

Do you make sure that the top is correct before you really start lengthening the outrun?

It really just depends on the situation: the kind of dog that I have, and the kind of sheep that I'm using. I have a young bitch now, about fourteen months old. Her sides are beautiful, her outruns are beautiful, but when I have heavy sheep out there she'll go tight at the top, and when I have light sheep she'll give them more space. But I'm working on it, because when you get to a trial with heavy sheep, you still want your dog deep enough so you can get a 20-10. So with her, all I need to do is to stand close to the sheep, and that's enough pressure for her to be right. With a dog that's really hard, really pushing, blasting in without any real feeling for the sheep, I'll start doing other things, like stopping the dog, going parallel, going a little past the dog toward the sheep, and then asking the dog around again. A lot of times that'll really work fine. Some dogs you need to get a little more aggressive with: lie them down, walk straight at them with a stick until they give ground to you, and then, once they do, ask them around again. If they come in again, stop them again, walk at them with a stick until they give, and then ask them for the flank again. If they get it right, back off right away and let them know that they're right, and pretty soon they'll start figuring it out.

How do you go about introducing the stop to your young dogs? Do you let the dog pick whether it wants to stand or to lie down?

I do. If the dog wants to stand, I'll teach him to stand first. I'll also teach him to lie down, but I'll do that when he's at my side. But when I ask dogs like that to stop at balance at the beginning, I'll say "stand" rather than "lie down."

When do you start insisting on absolute obedience with the stop, or with any of the commands?

You know, I think if you're smart about livestock and you allow the dog to be in control of the livestock, I don't think you ever really have to do that. You and the dog just become a team, because the dog trusts you and you trust the dog. So if you ask for a stop, and it makes sense to the dog, the dog is going to stop. There are times, of course, that you have to insist, with your panels and so on, but my dogs have saved me so many times at the panels—they have a lot more sense about it than I have. So if I give them a little flank and they're saying, "no, no, that's not right," I'll usually give in and not insist. There are times when I have to insist on something like a stop, but usually it isn't necessary.

What about the steady command? When do you introduce the idea of pace to the dogs that you're training?

That depends on the dog, too. If I have a dog that's a little reticent, I'll ask for more push. If I have a dog who's really pushing, I might run through the sheep a few times to get him thinking about where he's supposed to be, and where he's supposed to be taking the sheep. But I don't want to put a lot of pressure on a dog to slow down too soon. I want the dog to treat the sheep nicely, but I also want him to feel comfortable pushing. That's why I don't like to ask for the steady too soon in the course of training. Eventually I like to put a couple of different gears on my dogs.

How do you put those different gears on the dog?

Just with different amounts of pressure put on the dog. I use different versions of my stop whistle to slow the dog down, and I use a faster, more exciting walkup whistle to get the dog going faster with a little more push.

When do you start introducing whistles?

Again, that depends on the dog. But usually when they know their flanks, have a good stop, and may be driving a little bit. I don't start using flanks on the drive for awhile, but if they're responding well to all that, a lot of times they respond even better and more quickly if they have the whistles. So I start throwing the whistles in around then.

Do you teach all of your whistles to the dog at the same time?

I teach the stop and the walk-up first—usually they get those pretty quickly. I like them to be pretty solid on the voice commands of the flanks before I add in the whistle.

How about shedding? When do you start introducing that to your dogs?

Some dogs really love shedding, and you find that out the first time you introduce it to them. So I'd wait longer with dogs like that, because they want to shed when they're not supposed to be shedding. But in general I like to start it fairly soon, once the dog is comfortable with its flanks and is out-running about a hundred yards.

How do you start shedding with the dog?

I just take a big group (at least twenty or thirty sheep), make a big gap, and call the dog in. As soon as they're in the gap, I'll turn toward the group of sheep with heads facing me (as opposed to rears), and encourage the dog to turn the sheep and then walk them off. I want to give the dog a sense of what turning the sheep feels like.

What sorts of dogs would you want to start shedding with early?

A looser-eyed dog. My Jack dog loves to shed, so I had to back off on it a little with him. Dogs with a good amount of eye tend to like shedding better, in my experience.

Tell me about your early trial experiences with your dogs. What do you hope to get out of those trials?

Experience! I put some thought into the trials where I enter my young dogs; I wouldn't take a young dog out West and put him on range sheep for the first few trials. But the reason for the novice classes is to give the young dog experience, and that's what I try to get out of them. I don't expect to be competitive the first few times that I go: the young dogs can be great at home and then blow it big time once they're in a pressure situation. So I try to be humble, just let it happen, and make it the best experience it can possibly be.

What do you think about the Nursery program in general? Do you think it puts too much pressure on young dogs?

Well, the dogs have until they're three, and even if you bring a dog along slowly, I don't think it's really pushing them at that age. If it were a year younger, or even six months younger, I might think that it was a problem. But as it stands, I think it's really a good thing for the dogs. It's really helped to develop our breeding program in the United States. I just haven't seen that many dogs that are ruined by the Nursery program.

What tip would you like to pass on to people trying to train their own sheepdogs? What do you think is the most important thing for people to keep in mind?

Get some practical experience. If you have someone close by who has sheep and who will let you help with chores, with moving sheep, take them up on it. Practical work is very important in bringing a young dog along. The dog is going to learn to trust you if you understand and can read livestock and you allow that dog to keep the stock under control, without stopping him or flanking him at inappropriate times. That's ninety percent of it, really. So the sooner you get the feel for all that, for where the dog should be, the better. Most clinics are great experiences too, even if you're just sitting and watching. Find someone who can be your mentor, from whom you can learn what you need to learn.

Tom Wilson

GORDONSVILLE, VIRGINIA

A lifelong shepherd, Tom Wilson emigrated to the United States from Scotland in 1987. He and his dogs have proven to be successful teams on the North American trial scene since his arrival. Tom's Roy (whom he imported from Scotland as a puppy) was both a dominant force in trials (winning the Purina Outstanding Trial Dog Award in 1989) and an important sire in the bloodlines of working border collies in the United States and Canada. In recent years, Tom and his bitch Sly have won such major trials as Meeker (twice) and the Bluegrass Classic Stockdog Trial.

"You don't want them to be *too* easy when they're pups; you really want them to have enough of the rough edges."

How many new pups do you start a year?

Oh, it depends. Sometimes five, sometimes more than that, sometimes less. It depends on what bitches I like and just what comes up. But it's very seldom less than five.

What do you look for when you're choosing a puppy?

A good nature, to start with: friendly, not scared, not hyper.

Do you have a preference regarding the gender of the pup?

It doesn't matter.

Do you have a physical type that you prefer?

Yes. I like short-coupled dogs, and not too big.

How do you raise your puppies?

I try to socialize them as much as possible. I take them into the house, to be with them. I raise them to hear all the noises. I'd like to take them to trials, but it's not always possible or convenient to do that.

Do you let your pups follow you around as you're doing chores on your farm?

Yes. I let them come along with me from the very beginning, when they're very small. That way they can be with me, even if they're not interested in the sheep yet. It's good if they know their names at this point, so they'll come to you if you call them. Before they're interested in sheep, they can just be with me and not get into any trouble. And even later, when they *are* interested in the sheep a little bit, it doesn't do any harm to the older dog that's working to have the pup along.

When do you like pups to start showing an interest in sheep?

There's no set time. It's nice to see it from about four months on. If I don't see it by nine months or so, then I get worried. I don't want them to be *too* keen, but it's nice to know that there's something in there to work with.

Do you stop taking them with you to do chores once they're really keen?

Yes, at that point I stop, since they'd be in over their heads. They couldn't run fast enough if they needed to, and they could get hurt. I stop taking them when they start to interfere with the work.

How old are your pups when you actually start training them on sheep?

I've done it as young as four months, but six months upwards is more typical.

How big a field do you use when you start pups?

A flat field, with everything on it made easy for the dog. The size of the field wouldn't matter so much, since I use an older dog to help. I use something like a round pen, but I like to use older dogs (one or two) keeping back out of the way to do fence work to keep the sheep from escaping.

Do you find the pups are distracted by the older dog?

Yes, that can happen. But if you keep your older dog lying down, most puppies won't bother with it. If the dog has to move, the puppy might try to join in. It's just something you have to play around with and see how it goes. If the puppy is too keen on the older dog, you might not want to use it.

How many sheep do you use in those early training sessions?

Anywhere from ten to fifty—they're quieter in a group. I'd never use fewer than ten to start with. With a group that size, the sheep don't tend to run away as much, and they're not as focused on the pup.

Do you ever find that young dogs have trouble getting around so many sheep?

No, I don't. I think it's sometimes easier for you, because you sometimes can get to the other side without the pup seeing you doing it. Or you can go into the middle of the sheep and leave the pup on his own to figure things out. It's not just you and the pup; it's you, the sheep, and the pup.

How often do you train your young dogs?

Usually once a day for very short sessions (three to five minutes). Once I get started with a pup, I like to keep them going. But it doesn't have to be a rush job; I like the training situation to be just right. I might want to settle the sheep by working them with an older dog first, and then I'll bring the pup out after that.

What would you like to see with a promising pup in the first few sessions?

What I'm looking for most is a nice method, a pup who's thinking and not frightened. What I don't like is too much eye, a pup who's just glued on the sheep. If you use too few sheep you might get that sort of behavior a little bit more, and if you use more sheep you won't see it as much. I also don't like to see the tail up in excitement, with the pup rushing in. That can happen, and it might still be all right, but I'd rather not see it if I didn't have to. A pup that thinks, moves well, keeps his tail down, and doesn't show too much eye would be a very nice thing to see.

Is there anything that might happen in the first few sessions that might make you think that the dog just wasn't worth training at all?

No, not in the first few sessions. Not even in the first month. One thing that might not give you much hope is a dog that just didn't seem to have any method while working, or who didn't seem to have enough power or presence to move the stock. That would be scary, and that might make me think that the pup wasn't going to be able to come along.

What exactly do you mean by "method"?

The way the dog moves and approaches sheep, walks on to sheep, wants to be the boss over the sheep. The dog should want to cover the sheep when they start to break and should seem to enjoy having to do that. The opposite of all that would be a dog that tucks tail, runs away, barks, and doesn't want to look at the sheep. That would make me concerned.

What do you think is the easiest type of pup to train up?

One that moves correctly and wants to please you. It's hard to get everything together in one dog: a nice nature, not too much eye, good movement, willingness, listening well.

What sorts of dogs do you not enjoy working with?

One that lacks power would be the worst. If the dog didn't want to come near the sheep, or face the sheep, or was sulky if you talked to it, or didn't like pleasing you, I wouldn't want to work with it. You can waste a lot of time on dogs like that, and there are a lot of good dogs out there that don't have these problems. You can help dogs like that get better, but at the end of the day you're not going to have anything that you're really happy with.

Of all the dogs you've ever trained up, which one stands out in your mind as having been the easiest?

I trained my old Roy from six months, and he really does stand out in my mind as having been the easiest. We just started, we went out every day after that, and I didn't even feel that I really needed to train him.

So he obviously was a dog who actually lived up to that early promise.

He definitely did. That dog never seemed to need any correction—he just knew how to be in the right place at the right time.

Have you ever trained one that seemed that good early on but didn't live up to that early promise?

Oh, yes. You don't want them to be *too* easy when they're pups; you really want them to have enough of the rough edges. You also want to see some devilment and character when they're pups, enough challenge, to give you a better chance of ending up with a good dog at the end.

What are the stages of training that you use? What's your first stage of training, and what do you like the dog to master before moving on to the next stage?

The very first thing you want is for the dog to get to the other side of the sheep. In the beginning, I don't care *how* the dog gets there, but I want it willingly to get to the other side. After that you want to make sure that you're in the picture, and you want that dog to hold the sheep to you, however you move your body. Those are the first two most important things: the dog needs to get to the other side, and hold the sheep to you. The next thing is that you want that dog to come to you, to come off the stock: the dog has to know its name and come to me when I call, so we can begin again, and I'll let it go back to the sheep. At that point what you really have is a little outrun, if the dog is keen enough to go. That stage really continues for a long time. The next stage would be after the outrun gets longer (I'm talking around fifty yards), I work on the "steady": being on balance, treating the sheep nicely. Some dogs already have that sort of method and pace in them, and they pick it up easily. No dog can learn anything going a hundred miles an hour, so slowing the dog down is an important part of the next stage. At this point I like to see the dog thinking for itself and deciding to give the sheep a little space. After that we move on to flanks—I move my body to get the dog to one side or the other.

So you introduce the "steady" command fairly early?

Yes. Once the dog starts bringing me sheep about fifty yards away, I like to see some pace. I don't insist hard on it—the pup might bring the sheep in faster than an older dog would, but I don't want to see them racing the sheep.

How do you go about getting your pups to slow down?

I'll hold my hands up over the sheep as the dog fetches the sheep to me, catching their attention. If the dog doesn't get the idea from that, I might let the sheep go past me and tell the dog to "steady" as I bring the dog up to me. Some of them get the idea quickly, and some of them need a little more presence before you can get that steady. But I like the dog to understand "steady" long before I ever introduce a stop.

How do you go about lengthening and shaping the outrun?

Very gradually. Hundreds of outruns under fifty yards. Once they're doing fifty yards right, I try to do some seventy yards. I don't worry about pushing dogs off the stock for a long time, until they get their own idea that they should bring the sheep to me in a steady manner. Once they have that, the method should be there to allow them to give enough room at the top of their outrun. If they're not doing that, you might need to stop your dog back a bit and get in between the dog and the sheep to ask them to give more room at the top.

When do you first introduce whistles?

They have to be well broken to voice and working on the farm. My flank whistles come fairly early: once I have the dog responding to those and knowing what "steady" means, I'll start adding the stop with a voice command. After about a month of the voice command, I'll start adding in the stop whistle.

How do you go about introducing the stop?

I like the dog to be bringing sheep to me, and maybe doing a few flanks, before I start showing him the stop. I do it by having the dog bring the sheep up against a fence—the sheep can't go any farther, so they stop, and then the dog has to stop. That's when I first ask my dogs to stop.

So you don't teach a stop off livestock initially?

No, never.

Do you insist that the dog lies down on its belly when you give the stop command?

No, I ask for what the dog wants to do naturally. If it wants to stand, I say "stand." If it lies down that's what I ask it to do.

How do you go about teaching the drive?

I start that from pretty early on. As the dog fetches the sheep to me, maybe from fifty yards away, as the sheep are coming up to you, you just call the dog's name. As the dog comes to you, you can move your body a bit and walk. The sheep will move away; and if the dog takes a step or two, that's the beginning of the drive. That can be done within the first couple of months of the dog's training. You might get five yards at first, and then ten yards. You never force anything—the dog doesn't know a walk up command yet, you're just clicking your fingers at this point. All the dog knows is that it's brought you the sheep, and that it wants to go to the sheep again; you're just letting it go. If the dog wants to go to the side, you'll just say his name to hold him there, and if he stays behind the sheep for a second, that's good enough at this point. Then you might call the dog back and send him again.

When do you start insisting on absolute obedience in your commands? How do you balance the need for obedience with your desire to develop a natural, thoughtful dog?

It's a gradual thing—it's hard to say exactly *when* that happens. I'd say the dog is two years old and well broken before I really start insisting on obedience. But I might need to insist earlier if the dog had a fault that I wasn't prepared to live with, things like rushing in at the sheep, slicing the corners, biting at the sheep. Then I'd have to insist that the dog do what I say to prevent these sorts of things from occurring. But if I can get by, I'd rather let obedience go for awhile.

How early do you introduce shedding?

Fairly early. If I'm standing among twenty or thirty sheep and I call the dog to me, if it comes in that's the beginning of shedding. That's what I want to see at that stage: I want the dog to be able to come to me and not to be scared when it's coming through the sheep. I don't attempt the shed as such until the dog is bringing the sheep to me in a steady fashion. You'll get a feeling at that point that the dog is ready to progress, and at that point you might ask it to try to hold one of two big groups of sheep. But at that early stage, I'm not asking the dog to come in and hold one or two sheep against the pull of a big group. I'm talking about shedding maybe ten sheep one way and ten the other.

At what point do you like to start entering dogs in trials? How does trialing fit into your training program?

It's not really important to me. If I think the dog's capable, I don't mind doing it, and it's a good place to take them to find out exactly where you are in training, what you need to be learning, and what stage your dog is at. As long as the dog isn't over its head, with too big a course or too rough sheep, or too small a field with wild ping-pong sheep, it could be helpful. Some dogs reach the trialing stage more quickly than others, but I think most would start to benefit at around two years.

Do you have any advice for people training a dog, especially people training one for the first time?

I'd tell them to try to show the dog what to do, rather than demanding it of them. Be interested in your dog and the sheep, and understand what you're trying to accomplish. Watch the movements of the sheep. Don't expect too much; be satisfied with little stages, and things will progress more quickly. Don't get too focused on what you want to do: just go out, enjoy your dog, and the little things will soon start to develop into the bigger things.

Lightning Source UK Ltd.
Milton Keynes UK
UKOW02f0859021116
286648UK00002B/418/P